MW00584557

SPIRITUAL WARFARE
AND DIVINE MERCY

SPIRITUAL WARFARE AND DIVINE MERCY

The Weapons for Our Times

Fr. Ken Geraci, CPM

TAN Books

Gastonia, North Carolina

Imprimi Potest[1]: Very Rev. David M. Wilton, CPM
Superior General of the Fathers of Mercy
April 12, 2015
Divine Mercy Sunday
THE FATHERS OF MERCY
806 Shaker Museum Road
Auburn, KY 42206

Cover design by Caroline K. Green
Cover image: Sacred Heart of Jesus by stephendra/Shutterstock.

Library of Congress Control Number: 2023938342

ISBN: 978-1-5051-1433-1
Kindle ISBN: 978-1-5051-1434-8
ePUB ISBN: 978-1-5051-1435-5

Published in the United States by
TAN Books
PO Box 269
Gastonia, NC 28053
www.TANBooks.com

Printed in the United States of America

---

[1] This applies to the examination of conscience found in the back of the book.

In loving memory of John Moorehouse,
Catholic husband, father of five, and editor of TAN Books

CONTENTS

PREFACE

After several years of crisscrossing the United States as a mission preacher and retreat master, I have been tempted to set aside all of my preaching material and speak exclusively on the Rosary and the Divine Mercy Chaplet. Though a slightly impulsive sentiment, I believe we have entered some final chapters of our Faith that would merit such an action (*CCC* 675–677).

It is no surprise to anyone reading this book that the Catholic faith is suffering worldwide. My personal experience of the general cross-section of the Faith in America is that it has a grim outlook. There are only a few examples of dioceses in the United States that are flourishing, and even fewer countries that have been able to maintain and grow their Catholic identity. As a traveling missionary, it is rare that I find myself in a parish bursting with zealous parishioners. More often than not, I find myself at parishes in a state of attrition, where parishioners are mostly in their sixties and young families make up only a fraction of the congregation. Most of the faithful will tell us that it has been years since they have heard sermons on the Eucharist, sin, hell and the devil, the sacrament of Holy Matrimony, and other vital elements that make up our Faith. As clearly represented in our culture, the Faith is under siege. We are losing.

Do not take my word for it; simply examine your own experience with family and friends. Everywhere I go, without exception, people are asking for prayers for their family members or friends who have fallen away from the Faith. Far too many lament the fact that their children no longer practice their Catholic faith, or that their grandchildren have never received the sacraments or get to hear the Holy Name of Jesus and His teachings in their homes. Every one of us knows the pain of having those we love inch closer to eternal damnation because they have abandoned Jesus Christ and conformed themselves to the world.

When faced with these realities, it is easy to feel overwhelmed and helpless. However, we have been given weapons from heaven to battle against the powers of hell and *win*. War has been declared on us (see Rv 12:17), and we have two choices: surrender or fight.

When speaking on these subjects, there are those who are blindly optimistic. They say to me, "But Father, what's the big deal? I have read the last chapter of the Bible and we win!" To which I simply retort, *"But what is the score?"* Did your children make it to the winning side? Did your loved ones make it? What about our enemies or those who persecuted us; where are they?" Our Lady of Fatima tells us that souls are falling into hell like snowflakes in winter because there is no one to offer prayers or sacrifices for them.

This book hopes to open our minds to the reality of spiritual warfare and the role the Divine Mercy message can play in your victory. It will open our minds to a greater awareness of the assaults of the devil and the weapons we have at our disposal to combat him. This journey will help to inform and equip you to engage in this battle, to protect ourselves and our loved ones, and to rescue souls that have fallen into darkness.

This book will begin with a basic overview of spiritual warfare, followed by an outline of the spiritual weapons we have available, specifically as it relates to the four weapons given to us by Jesus through the Divine Mercy message. The most important chapters will be on the Divine Mercy Chaplet as an extension of the Liturgy of the Eucharist, the Sacrifice of the Mass, and how the Chaplet of Divine Mercy makes present the graces of Calvary. For many of you, this teaching will be new and enable you to pray the Chaplet with greater intentionality, vigor, and power. We are fighting not only for our own souls when we pray but for *those of the whole world.*

Like my previous book, *Why Be Catholic?*, this book is an adaptation of the preaching and conferences I have given over the years. It is my sincere hope to expand your knowledge of spiritual warfare and help equip you for the battle so that one day you may look upon the Face of God.

An Introduction to Saint Faustina and the Divine Mercy Devotion

Some of my readers may already be familiar with the story of Saint Faustina Kowalska and the Divine Mercy Devotion, but others may not. Still others may simply need a refresher. While I will of course go into more detail in the chapters that follow, it is probably prudent here to introduce you to this wonderful Polish nun and the devotion that Christ instituted through her; a devotion that has swept across the world in the last half-century.[2]

Maria Faustina (birth name Helena) Kowalska was born on August 25, 1905, in Glogowiec, Poland, into a Catholic family. She was always an ordinary girl: a good daughter, sibling, and friend. Yet, there was a particular set of graces dwelling in her soul that gave her a deeper spiritual sensitivity than others. At the age of seven, Helena first felt the promptings towards religious life. Around the age of eighteen, Helena approached her parents about entering the convent; for whatever reason, her parents were adamantly against the idea and denied her permission to pursue religious life. Discouraged and hurt by this, she tried to drown

---

[2] If you feel you are already sufficiently familiar with this background, feel free to skip ahead to chapter 1.

1

out her calling by immersing herself in the vain things of life. But in July of 1924, while at a dance with friends, in the midst of the crowded room and music, Jesus Christ appeared to her. We read in her diary:

> While everybody was having a good time, my soul was experiencing deep torments. As I began to dance, I suddenly saw Jesus at my side, Jesus racked with pain, stripped of His clothing, all covered with wounds, who spoke these words to me: **How long shall I put up with you and how long will you keep putting Me off?**[3] At that moment the charming music stopped, [and] the company I was with vanished from my sight; there remained Jesus and I. (*Diary* 9)

Helena faked a headache, then excused herself from the dance and went directly to the Cathedral of Saint Stanislaus Kostka. There she prostrated herself in prayer and asked Our Lord for guidance: "Then I heard these words: **Go at once to Warsaw; you will enter a convent there.** I rose from prayer, came home, and took care of things that needed to be settled. As best I could, I confided to my sister what took place within my soul. I told her to say good-bye to our parents, and thus, in my one dress, with no other belonging, I arrived in Warsaw" (*Diary* 10).

In July of 1924, acting in great faith, Helena traveled to Warsaw, where Our Lord guided her to a confessor who helped her find basic accommodations while she searched

---

[3] Throughout Faustina's diary, quoted often in this book, Christ's words appear in bold, and the Blessed Virgin Mary's in italics.

for a convent. Visiting numerous convents, she was turned away from them all. "Sorrow gripped my heart, and I said to the Lord Jesus, 'Help me; don't leave me alone.' At last, I knocked on our door [of the Congregation of the Sisters of Our Lady of Mercy]" (*Diary* 13).

Though Helena received her initial acceptance into the Congregation of the Sisters of Our Lady of Mercy, there was still the matter of a dowery. As a result of World War I, the economic situation in Poland was dire. Convents could not afford to take in a member without some sort of financial support being paid. To raise the necessary money, Helena took a job as a "domestic" (nanny and house keeper) for the Lipszyc family near Warsaw. She was beloved by the family and noted as a dedicated worker. After nearly a year of service, Helena was able to cover her costs to enter religious life; she officially applied and was accepted into the congregation on August 1, 1925. Nine months later, on April 30, 1926, Helena received the habit of the congregation and was given the name Sister Maria Faustina.

Initially, Sr. Faustina's religious experience was relatively normal. She was a sister of the second choir, which relegated her to kitchen duties and manual labor, all of which she was very accustomed to and did the work with great joy. She loved the periods of prayer and even longed for greater opportunities for it. This temptation, along with other spiritual oppression, caused Sr. Faustina to consider leaving her convent for another. But Divine Providence willed that she stay: "I saw the very sorrowful Face of Jesus. There were open wounds on His Face, and large tears were falling on my bedspread. Not knowing what all this meant, I asked

Jesus, 'Jesus, who has hurt You so?' And Jesus said to me, **It is you who will cause Me this pain if you leave this convent. It is to this place that I called you and nowhere else; and I have prepared many graces for you.** I begged pardon of Jesus and immediately changed my decision" (*Diary* 19).

The darkness grew and lasted approximately one year. On April 16, 1928, two weeks prior to her first vows, she received a gift of divine love that lifted her from her darkness and allowed her to forget her past sufferings.

Once in vows, Faustina worked in the kitchen and carried out various duties in the congregation and with various houses. Though often overcome with illness, she served wherever she was needed with great joy and love. In addition, Sr. Faustina lived an austere lifestyle with extensive fasts. This is reminiscent of the life of Bernadette Soubirous, the visionary from Lourdes. Saint Bernadette received visions of the Blessed Virgin Mary, who announced to the world that she is "the Immaculate Conception." The Blessed Mother gave the world a place of pilgrimage to her Son and also a place of healing. Because Bernadette was "chosen" to receive these revelations, the common world thought her to be a living saint, but she knew better. Bernadette entered the convent, where she conformed herself to the rule of the congregation and sanctified her daily duties through prayer. Bernadette was not made a saint because of the visions and revelations; she was made a saint because she loved, prayed, obeyed, and suffered with great zeal for souls. In short, she conformed her life to Christ. Sr. Faustina set out on a similar path. "Neither graces, nor revelations, nor raptures, nor gifts granted to a soul make it perfect, but rather the intimate union of the soul with God. . . . My sanctity and perfection is based upon the close union of my will with the will of God" (*Diary* 1107).

On the evening of February 22, 1931, Jesus appeared to Sr. Faustina and asked her to paint an image according to the pattern she saw, with the signature, "Jesus, I trust in You" (*Diary* 47). It was at this point that the Divine Mercy Image was first introduced to Sr. Faustina. After her perpetual vows, she was sent to Vilnius, Poland, where Our Lord placed her under the spiritual direction of Fr. Michael Sopocko. Though mostly illiterate, Sr. Faustina was directed to write down all of the messages she received from Jesus. Father Sopocko, convinced of the importance of what was happening, assisted Sr. Faustina in this labor of Mercy. It took until January 1934 for the two to find an artist who was able to paint the image according to Faustina's directives. This unlikely team began gathering fuel for a fire that soon would ignite the world ablaze with the Mercy of God.

At this point in Sr. Faustina's religious vocation, the extraordinary and supernatural had manifested in the fullest sense, giving her a "call-within-a-call." This vocation to be the "Secretary of my Mercy" (*Diary* 965, 1160, 1605) and to "prepare the world for [Jesus'] final coming" (*Diary* 429) was lived in and through the ordinary life of a sister in the Congregation of the Sisters of Our Lady of Mercy. Faustina did not spend her days in visions and ecstasies but rather in fidelity to the rule and her daily duties. It is amongst the ordinary that the extraordinary begins to come alive. There are countless twists and turns in this journey, but God is working through them all. On more than one occasion the entire project was in total jeopardy of failing. Whether it was the angel (of Satan) who enticed Sr. Faustina to burn her diary, or the near arrest of Father Sopocko by the Gestapo, or the condemnation of the visions by the Church, God used these two as His instruments to prepare the world for His second coming by granting the world this last hour of Mercy.

Saint Faustina would die of tuberculosis on October 5, 1938, just thirteen years after entering the convent. At the time of her death, she had no idea of the legacy she had left behind and all that would be written about the Divine Mercy and about her life. However, the devotion she tried so hard to spread was not immediately met with open arms.

Two decades after her death, in 1959, the Vatican placed a ban on the Divine Mercy Image and messages from Faustina's writings. This ban, or condemnation, was directly related to the unavailability of the original documentation, inaccuracies in translations from Polish to Italian, and an inadequate theological commentary on it all. The condemnations of the revelations left Father Sopocko shunned and in isolation. Unable to preach on the revelations given to Sr. Faustina, Father Sopocko threw himself into the historical study of God's Divine Mercy; from the Sacred Scriptures, from patristic sources, and from Divine Liturgy. This study would prove to further refine and authenticate the revelations. Father Sopocko was always obedient, yet he did not stop trying to fulfill his mission.

One day, in the summer of 1965, he had an opportunity to meet with Karol Wojtyla, the archbishop of Kraków. Wojtyla was fascinated by Sr. Faustina's writings. Three months after that meeting, Wojtyla took up the case with the cardinal of the Congregation of the Doctrine of the Faith, who set in motion the informative process to vet and authenticate the writings of Sr. Faustina and the message of Divine Mercy. Sadly, ten years after the informative process of verifying the revelations began, on February 15, 1975, Father Sopocko died.

After careful investigation, on April 15, 1978, the Vatican lifted the ban on the Divine Mercy Image and the writings of Sr. Maria Faustina Kowalska. Six months later, Karol Wojtyla was elected to the papacy. Now John Paul II, he would bring into full light the message of Divine Mercy. John Paul II had the privilege of canonizing Sr. Maria Faustina Kowalska on April 30, 2000, the first saint of the new millennium. (Fr. Michael Sopocko would be declared Blessed by Benedict XVI on September 28, 2009.) The Holy Father also established an official feast dedicated to Divine Mercy in the liturgical calendar, which falls on the second Sunday after Easter. Pope John Paul II would even find himself as the fulfillment of a prophecy found in the diary: "**I bear a special love for Poland, and if she will be obedient to My will, I will exalt her in might and holiness. From her will come forth the spark that will prepare the world for My final coming**" (*Diary* 1732).

Saint Faustina was the secretary and prophetess of God's Mercy, while Blessed Sopocko was the laborer, and John Paul II was that *spark* that set the world on fire with God's Love. But in our modern day, love has grown cold. Much of humanity has turned away from God's commandments and teachings. The Church is in crisis—basic doctrine is questioned, churches are filled with compromise, and bishop is set against bishop and cardinal against cardinal. The smoke of Satan, as Pope Paul VI said, has very much permeated the Church and the world. There is no place to hide, and the declaration of war from the book of Revelation is more obvious today than ever before: "Then the dragon was angry with the woman, *and went off to make war on the rest of her offspring*, on those who keep the commandments of God and bear testimony to Jesus" (Rv 12:17, emphasis added). War has been declared; the only question is: Will you fight?

PART I

THE BASICS OF BATTLE

CHAPTER 1

AN OVERVIEW OF SPIRITUAL WARFARE

"Then the dragon was angry with the woman, and went off to make war on the rest of her offspring, on those who keep the commandments of God and bear testimony to Jesus."

—Revelation 12:17

Recognizing the Battle

One of the main principles of spiritual warfare—that war has been declared on us by forces that seek our eternal damnation—is reinforced by the Scriptures:

> Be sober, be watchful. Your adversary the devil prowls around like a roaring lion, seeking someone to devour. (1 Pt 5:8)

> For we are not contending against flesh and blood, but against the principalities, against the powers, against the world rulers of this present darkness, against the spiritual hosts of wickedness in the heavenly places. (Eph 6:12)

> We know that we are of God, and the whole world is in the power of the evil one. (1 Jn 5:19)

> The thief comes only to steal and kill and destroy; I
> came that they may have life, and have it abundantly.
> (Jn 10:10)

Recognizing that war has been declared on us is imperative for a Christian to internalize. Failure to do so will increase the likelihood that you live a misunderstood Christian life and/or become a casualty of the war. A *misunderstood Christian life* is where an individual believes that if he says his prayers and does all the things asked of by Jesus, all will be well. This is a dangerous mindset to adopt. We cannot take such an important war so casually. Just as in a natural war, the enemy is constantly looking for opportunities to attack and will sabotage your best and most perfect efforts. The Gospel of Matthew tells us: "The kingdom of heaven is like a man who sowed good seed in his field. But while everyone was asleep, his enemy came and sowed weeds among the wheat, and slipped away. When the wheat sprouted and bore grain, then the weeds also appeared" (Mt 13:24–26).

There are many times in life when people will become angry with God, especially when something tragic happens or does not go the way we feel it should go. It always baffles me when someone is angry with God rather than channeling his anger toward sin or the diabolic. This goes to show how great our lack of awareness is and how effective the devil is at remaining in the shadows to conduct his clandestine war on mankind.

It is vitally important that we avoid extremes when it comes to spiritual warfare. Just as it is dangerous to see the devil around every corner and blame Satan as the cause of all our problems, it's also extremely dangerous to be so naive as to go through life failing to acknowledge the reality of the diabolic. Proper balance and discernment are necessary to keep ourselves in check.[4]

The Path to Victory: Communion with Christ and His Church

When considering our own individual strength and power in this war, we must acknowledge that *apart from [Jesus we] can do nothing* (Jn 15:5). With this said, the first principle of spiritual warfare is to stay with Jesus by staying in His Church. By being intentional in exercising our faith, Christ Himself will defend us and fight for us, as will the saints and angels. When we are in a state of grace, we are in communion with Christ and His Church. Just like in any good family or group of friends, there is strength and protection in numbers. Conversely, if we stray from "the pack," we set ourselves up to be picked off by a predator.

So the first question we need to ask ourselves is: Am I living my Catholic faith? Am I in the state of grace? Do I makes use of sacramentals? Am I with the Church or the world? Am I an American-Catholic or am I a Catholic-American?

An American-Catholic is one who sets his Catholic faith as one thing among many in his worldview, on the same

---

[4] There is a meme floating around the internet that says, "All things happen for a reason. Sometimes that *reason* is our bad decisions." To determine whether or not something is of the self, God, the evil one, natural causes, or a mix, one can turn to Saint Ignatius of Loyola's rules for discernment of spirits. Though this topic is outside the scope of this book, it is worth mentioning and considering for future study.

plane as his politics, profession, and hobbies. His faith simply influences his American citizenship and ideology. For a Catholic-American, however, his natural citizenship is animated and directed by his supernatural citizenship in heaven. Central to his life is the belief that he is a child of almighty God who is called to follow His divine revelation, His morality, and His natural law. His Catholic faith is *the* determining factor in his life and he lives in the world, but not of it.

Fr. John Malloy, one of our deceased priests of the Fathers of Mercy, would preach on what he called "but Catholics." He mourned how the Church was full of those who accept compromise, those who say "I'm Catholic, *but* . . ." Fill in the blank from there: " . . . but I think I should be able to take birth control"; " . . . but I support a woman's right to choose"; " . . . but I want to live with my girlfriend." Father Malloy would say we are going to hell on our proverbial buts!

We need the one, holy, catholic, and apostolic Church. Holy Mother Church is our key to victory. And, sometimes, in the event of paranormal activity, our Protestant neighbors prove this point. I have had more than one phone call from a non-Catholic asking for assistance in relation to paranormal activity in a home; where shadows move, children see deceased people, or sacred images or objects move on their own in their home. Yes, when things get diabolic and strange, people abandon *sola scriptura* and go searching for a Catholic priest with a crucifix, exorcism prayers, and a bucket of holy water!

The primary way of engaging in spiritual warfare is to stay in a state of grace, by aligning yourself with the fullness of the Faith found in the Catholic Church. This is minimally accomplished by keeping the precepts of the Church (*CCC* 2041):

- On Sundays and holy days of obligation, attend Mass and rest from servile labor.
- Confess your mortal sins at least once a year.
- Receive the sacrament of the Eucharist at least once during the Easter season.
- Observe the days of fasting and abstinence from meat established by the Church.
- Help provide for the needs of the Church.

Furthermore, every baptized person has as a universal call to holiness[5] that is lived out through the sanctification of their daily activities and prayer. One *must* exercise a personal relationship with God through prayer and by taking time each day to nourish his faith life and to ensure he is staying closer to God than to the world. A person must also take his vocation seriously and live it according to the mind of Jesus Christ, as expressed through His Church. Lastly, we must live out our vocations in the world through the proclamation of the Gospel (with or without words), including through the discipling of others when the situation calls for it, and by serving the needs of those in our community. Living these basic principles of Christianity will ensure that you are staying close to Jesus, and He and His Church are remaining close to you.

---

[5] See *Lumen Gentium*, chapter V.

These are the *ordinary* means of salvation found through Jesus Christ and His one, holy, catholic, and apostolic Church. By aligning ourselves as faithfully and closely to the fullness of truth found in the Catholic Church as we can, we help ensure our eternal salvation. This does not mean the mystical power and mystery of the sacraments is "ordinary"—quite the opposite! What we mean is that the Church offers us everyday actions that we are capable of carrying out (going to Mass, praying, reading Scripture, etc.). This is different from what we would call *extraordinary* means of salvation, which comes to us through God's mercy. We can receive God's mercy despite doing nothing to merit it. It is supernatural grace that draws us to Him. And even those outside the Church can experience His mercy. This is because while mankind is bound by our covenant relationship with God and the divine mandates attached to it, God is not. He is free to work out our salvation by whatever means He chooses. As Catholics, we believe that every human person ever created has the opportunity for eternal salvation, even if they have never heard the Holy Name of Jesus. God is as close to them as He is to us, and He desires their salvation just as strongly. Every day, God pours out *actual grace* upon those who do not know Him to help these individuals seek the good and avoid the bad. But for those of us who do know Him and have been received into His Church, there is a greater responsibility to respond to that opportunity. We have no excuse not to know what God expects of us. "To whom much is given, much be required" (Lk 12:48).

The Church: Cruise Ship or War Ship?

When speaking of the Church, she is often referred to as a ship or boat that sails upon the sea of time, journeying towards her heavenly homeland. I like this analogy because it gives us an opportunity to define what kind of vessel we are traveling on: Is it a *cruise ship* or a *war ship*? This is an important question to consider. The answer will help us identify our role upon this ship as we travel. If the vessel of the Church is a cruise liner that sets sail upon the ascension of Jesus Christ, then those aboard the ship are passengers and customers of a cruise. A passenger like this can have expectations of "receiving" and being "waited on" while aboard the cruise liner. However, if the vessel is a war ship, then those aboard are not passengers but crew members who will each have responsibilities and duties to perform. There will also be a culture of readiness on deck in the event we come under attack.

This question of the type of vessel we are on is relevant to the topic of spiritual warfare because it helps us set expectations for what is to come. Earlier in this chapter, I spoke of a *misunderstood Christian life*. Those who have this misunderstanding will often fall into the "cruise liner mentality" where they expect to be served rather than serve and sacrifice. When faced with storms and turbulent waters, a cruise liner (or one with a *misunderstood Christian life*) seeks to navigate away from and around the difficulties. Conversely, the war ship goes *into battle* with weapons and warriors ready for whatever may transpire. Whether we know it or not, we are those warriors that Jesus Christ has called to battle for souls.

Keeping with this analogy, I would like to give four simple rules for us to follow while aboard:

1. Follow the captain's orders.
2. Know your job and do it with excellence.
3. While doing your job, look to see if you can assist others.
4. Do not sink your own ship or shoot at your crewmates!

Let's take each of these one at a time.

Following the captain's orders: This is a call to live your faith. However, one cannot live his faith if he does not know or study it. In this analogy, the Captain is Jesus Christ and our "orders" are the divine mandates given to us through the Church. We cannot love what we do not know, which is why Saint Jerome would say, "Ignorance of Scripture is ignorance of Christ." Thus, living our faith is a constant cycle of learning, internalizing, living, loving, and sharing. We are not all called to be theologians, but we *are* all called to know the basics of the Faith. This is easily accomplished by spending time reading and praying the Sacred Scriptures, studying the *Catechism of the Catholic Church*, or reading/viewing different credible Catholic content online. By studying the official teachings of the Catholic Church, it will help keep us from error and sin. This is desperately needed right now, as we are living in a time of great malformation and compromise, even among the clergy and religious. If we do not know the captain or the orders, it is not possible to follow them. There is so much more to Catholicism than just saying a few prayers and going to Mass on Sundays. The greater our exposure to the teachings of Jesus Christ, the greater the opportunity is for us to experience Jesus Christ.

Know your job and do it with excellence: Live your vocation heroically. As referenced earlier, there are various vocations we are called to. The first vocation is the universal call to holiness, while the second is a particular vocation towards holy matrimony, priesthood, or religious life. Then, there are vocations within a vocation; the best example of this is the vocation of being a mother or father, which is a vocation within the vocation of Matrimony. For the laity who are married with children, their vocation(s) look like this:

1. Universal call to holiness – Living your sonship or daughterhood in Christ
2. Holy Matrimony – Living your covenant relationship with your spouse according to the mind of Jesus Christ and His Church
3. Parents to your children – Raising and forming your children in the Holy Spirit and teachings of Jesus Christ and not of the world.

These three vocations are then lived out in the "mission field" (the geographic community) in which we find ourselves. Knowing our vocation and living it with excellence is *not* intuitive; we must commit to studying and living God's plan for marriage and God's plan for parenting. Life should be lived in that order: God, marriage, children. It is a common reality that the children take over and dominate our time and attention. When this happens for prolonged periods, neglect can set in and your marriage can start to fall apart.

While doing your job, look to see if you can assist others:
This is the call to a life of service within the mission field of
your life. Christianity is not exclusively about your personal
relationship with Jesus Christ alone. Rather, we are called to
live lives of service within our covenant family, caring for the
needs of the entire Body of Christ as best as we are able. This
concept of service is best expressed by living out the Spiritual
and Corporal Works of Mercy.

The Spiritual Works of Mercy	The Corporal Works of Mercy
• Admonish the sinner.	• Feed the hungry.
• Instruct the ignorant.	• Give drink to the thirsty.
• Counsel the doubtful.	• Clothe the naked.
• Comfort the sorrowful.	• Visit the imprisoned.
• Bear wrongs patiently.	• Shelter the homeless.
• Forgive all injuries.	• Visit the sick.
• Pray for the living and the dead.	• Bury the dead.

Just as we have been discipled in our faith, so we are called
to disciple others. Remember the words or Our Lord:
"What you did for the least of my brethren you did for me"
(Mt 25:40).

Do not sink your own ship or shoot at your crewmates!
Throughout the history of the Church, she has sailed on both
smooth and turbulent waters. However, the place we find
ourselves today is some of the most turbulent times in world
history. The Universal Church is being attacked from both
external and internal forces. In terms of the internal conflict,

the Church is being rocked from both the Left and the Right. This is not just about one particular issue. Rather, there are those on the Left who wish to liberate the Deposit of Faith from the Church and conform and submit it to the world. The elevation of Marxist ideologies, such as identity politics and certain social justice issues, are deemed equivocal to—if not even more important than—issues surrounding the taking of innocent human life through abortion and euthanasia. These issues have enculturated their way into the Church to such a degree that we see *bishop opposing bishop, cardinal against cardinal, and churches full of those who accept compromise.*[6] There is a danger that these ideologies have become idols.

On the alt-right, we find those who reject Vatican II and the authority of the Church in various areas. This small group subverts the faithful by sowing seeds of doubt and undermines the legitimate authority of the Church. One of the devil's greatest accomplishments in spiritual warfare is to get the "crew" to fight each other and damage its own vessel, placing our attention on each other rather than our common enemy.

As a traveling confessor and mission preacher, it becomes more and more difficult to lead the faithful into the truths of our Faith when they are constantly being undermined by various clergy, religious, Church leadership, and various laity. To fight against this, we must unleash the Truth, but not the sharpness of our tongues. We must pray, fast, and do penance, but not gossip and murmur. We should look at the examples of the heroic leadership in our Church, such as

---

[6] John Ata, "A Message from Our Lady - Akita, Japan: EWTN," *EWTN Global Catholic Television Network*, November 2011, https://www.ewtn.com/catholicism/library/message-from-our-lady--akita-japan-5167.

Cardinal Raymond Burke, Cardinal Janis Pujats, Archbishop Tomasz Peta, Archbishop Jan Paweł Lenga, and Bishop Athanasius Schneider, who came together to help rectify the forty most common errors in the life of the Church today by issuing a declaration addressing each issue.[7] The way we fight against those who teach and promote error is to address the issue, not the person. Calling people names and participating in other personal attacks does not build up the Body of Christ; rather, it tears it down. Remember the nine ways of participating in the sins of another (*CCC* 1868):

- By counsel
- By command
- By consent
- By provocation
- By praise or flattery
- By concealment
- By partaking
- By silence
- By defense of a sinful action

When popular evangelists or YouTube personalities post vehement attacks against others, especially bishops, cardinals, or the Holy Father, we can participate in those sins by viewing or sharing their content. Rather, we must follow Our Lord's direction to Saint Faustina "to shun murmurers" like the plague.[8] There is no sin in dealing with the

---

[7] Cardinal Raymond Burke, Cardinal Raymond Leo, et al. "Declaration of the Truths Relating to Some of the Most Common Errors in the Life of the Church of Our Time," *RORATE CAELI*, 31 May 2019, https://rorate-caeli.blogspot.com/2019/06/for-record-declaration-of-truths.html.

[8] Kowalska, Maria Faustina. *Diary of Saint Maria Faustina Kowalska:*

subject matter itself, only when making it derogatorily personal. Sometimes it is necessary to identify the person that has given scandal through his behavior or teaching, but the contents of the rebuttal must be restricted to the teaching at hand and not focus on fault finding or name calling of the individual.

If we keep focusing on each other's sins and failings, we will be caught up with fighting each other rather than fighting the diabolic. It distracts us and weakens our ability to fight who we should be fighting. We have to bring ourselves back to the reality that we are under siege and that the one attacking is Satan, who is "a murderer and a liar" (Jn 8:44); he will use any and all means to keep the attention off of him. It is said that Satan's greatest accomplishment is to make souls believe he does not exist. This is an opportunity for us to bring the spiritual war into greater focus and engage it more fully. In doing so, we will protect ourselves and our loved ones. As faithful and obedient Catholics, we will participate in driving the diabolic back and regain many souls that have fallen.

In this opening chapter, I have tried to help you realize the battle you are in. We cannot win a war if we do not know we are in one. Once we have opened our eyes to the reality of the danger all around us, we must realize our best means to win is by remaining in communion with Jesus Christ and His Church. With these basic lessons learned, let us move forward and discuss our prayer life more specifically and how it is one of the greatest weapons God has given us to defeat our enemy.

Divine Mercy in My Soul. (Stockbridge: Marian Press, 1987), 1760.

CHAPTER 2

SPIRITUAL WARFARE AND OUR PRAYER LIFE

A Holistic Approach

As it applies to spiritual warfare, the key principles are to (1) realize that we are in a spiritual battle and (2) be sure that your daily life is oriented towards keeping yourself safe while engaged in this battle, which is done primarily by living in communion with the Holy Catholic Church. It is God's Mercy that envelops, protects, and empowers us to engage in this battle; this is why the first chapter was dedicated to making sure we are living our covenant relationship within the Most Holy Trinity, by staying in the Church. This book will soon transition into describing the weapons given us by Jesus through the Divine Mercy message, but we must first lay the groundwork to ensure we are engaging in this spiritual battle *holistically*, making sure the weapons of Divine Mercy are integrated into the wholeness of our spiritual lives rather than just being accessories. This second stage of spiritual warfare will help us ensure our own personal house is in order. To check one's inventory, the following questions must be asked:

1. Am I in the state of grace?
2. Do I have a daily plan of prayer?

3. Do I have a monthly goal for receiving the sacraments?

   • Commitment for a regular confession? Always attend Sunday Mass and look for the opportunity to attend a daily Mass occasionally throughout the month?

4. Do I have a plan for various forms of bodily/corporeal mortification?

   • Such as fasting from food, abstinence from entertainment, willful denial of pleasures, deliberately inconveniencing oneself?

5. Do I have a specific intention to engage in service to my community?

These are all key elements of a person's life to assist him in the spiritual war: receiving grace through the sacraments, nurturing a relationship with God through prayer, forming spiritual discipline through penance, and serving others as God commands us to (which also tampers our own self-love). Let us discuss each of these briefly.

Am I in a State of Grace?

In the movies and comic books, you never see a superhero running around in blue jeans and a t-shirt. Instead, they always have a superhero outfit on. For anyone who remembers the movie *The Incredibles*, there is a memorable scene where a robot is destroying the city, and the character Frozone is scurrying around trying to get ready for battle, but he cannot find his superhero outfit. He runs around yelling to his wife,

"Honey, where is my super suit?" This may be a bit cheesy, but being in a state of grace is the Christian's version of a super suit. Not super in the sense of natural powers but rather supernatural powers, in the sense that the power of Jesus Christ, through the Holy Spirit, acts in and through us. Being in a state of grace also protects us from the assaults of the devil. This is the base layer of the armor of God (Eph 6:11–18).

Do I Have a Daily Plan of Prayer?

When I worked in the business world, we had a saying: "If you cannot measure something, you cannot manage that thing." This principle can easily be applied to our prayer lives. Most people I encounter on my missions have a very intuitive prayer life, whereby they pray well throughout the week, but there is no rhyme or reason to what and how they pray. There are always a few staples—Mass on Sunday, grace before meals, devotionals or a Rosary from time to time—but very little structure. There is a difference between *a person of prayer* and *a person who prays.*

The difference between the two can be summarized as committed versus casual. A *person of prayer* is dedicated to a life of prayer. If, for some reason, particular prayers are not said, or there is a busy day that prevents him from his normal routine of prayer, he feels like he has missed out on something; much like a husband or wife who, upon traveling for a few days, is taken away from the routine of communion with his or her family. A *person who prays* will say prayers throughout his day or week, but is not attentive to the commitment of daily communion through those prayers.

Developing a daily prayer routine is invaluable to a person's life because it is a commitment of an individual to give his time back to God. One of the most valuable things we have is time. Think of how precious our time is. We must ask an important question: How much of this precious commodity is dedicated to God? If we take the biblical principle of tithing, giving back 10 percent and adjusting for when we sleep, we would want to give approximately twelve hours per week to God. If all we give Him is a handful of prayers during the week and Mass on Sunday, we may think or feel that we are honoring God, but in reality, we are not giving God what He is due. And to be clear, He does not want this time from us because it benefits Him or He needs it; He wants this time with us *because He knows it benefits us*. Failing to dedicate time back to God could be a sign of selfishness or the sinful wasting of time. In developing a one-hour daily plan of prayer (in addition to Sunday Mass), you will be giving yourself back to God in an intentional and committed way. You will also set a foundation for growth and development in the spiritual life. One of the most effective ways of growing in the spiritual life is to develop a plan for success, and because prayer is the cornerstone of our relationship with God, it is best to start there.

Recommended components of a *daily* plan of prayer would include:

- Informal prayer
- Formal prayer (20–30 minutes)
- Scripture (10 minutes)
- Silence (15 minutes)
- Continuing education/formation (15 minutes)

The most effective way of developing a daily plan of prayer is to actually pray through this process. We should sit with Jesus in the Blessed Sacrament and ask Him, "Lord, what formal prayers are you inviting me to say? How much Scripture? How much silence? What books/content are you calling me to look at?" The goal is to develop a plan of prayer that pairs with what God is inviting us towards and not our own ideas. It may also be a good idea to run it past your pastor, or a religious or established lay person noted for having some formation in the spiritual life. Having your plan checked out will help avoid excess or laxity and create greater opportunity for success. Once a plan is in place, at the end of each day or week, you can reflect back on your success or failures and make the necessary adjustments for the week to come. A daily plan should grow and develop over the years. It would be unfortunate if your plan is the same today as it was five years ago.

Informal Prayer

Informal prayer is simply our conversation with God. This is exercising our covenant relationship in the Blood of Jesus Christ and will keep us close to God. I love the Protestant question, "Do you have a personal relationship with Jesus Christ?" Being the people of the Eucharist, we have a *very* developed answer to that question, but with that said, this question points towards the notion of talking with Jesus throughout our day and inviting Him into the regular moments of our daily lives. This perspective is in fact very Catholic. This notion of exercising a personal relationship with God throughout our day parallels Saint Thérèse of Lisieux's "little way" of doing small things with great love. This entails simply offering up little moments of our day to the glory of God and for the salvation of souls. Anything from doing the dishes to serving those in need to just conversing with Jesus as a friend qualify as forms of informal prayer. Sometimes our little, quick, and informal prayers are called "javelin prayers," little petitions and acts of adoration and thanksgiving we hurl up to God at any moment. In short, all elements of our day can be sanctified and turned into little acts of prayer.

There is no amount of time one needs to set for informal prayer, but we do need to examine ourselves at the end of the day to see how our informal communication has been. Informal prayer will/should be a larger part of our day, not necessarily because of the amount of time we spend on it but because of the quality of those interactions and conversations. An example of this would be a husband and wife with several children; they may not have hours of alone time to talk and share in each other's day, but a loving couple maximizes the small amounts of time in sharing the joys, difficulties, sorrows, and highlights of the day by being present to each other and intentional in those moments of communication.

In addition to sanctifying our daily duties, we can maximize our conversations with Jesus throughout the day by speaking to Him in three ways: as our friend, as our Savior, and as our King. Speaking to Jesus as a friend is basic and intuitive; this is just generic conversation that might also include a few emotional moments. Speaking to Jesus as our

Savior means standing at the foot of the cross with Mother
Mary and Saint John and looking at Jesus who has been
crucified, speaking to Him from your heart of the sorrow for
your sins and those of the whole world, keeping him company in His suffering, abandonment, and abasement. And,
lastly, in speaking to Jesus as King, you will have to use your
imagination for a moment. Imagine walking into the greatest throne room of a King that ever existed, with servants
and members of the King's court present. How would you
approach the King? Some of us may run the other way out
of a feeling of fear or gross inferiority. However, we have to
recognize that the King has summoned us into His presence
because He wants our company. So, how would you speak to
the King of kings and Lord of lords? We would bow down,
we would speak in the greatest praise and reverence, and we
would recognize His majesty and royal dignity. By speaking
to the King, by receiving His favor, we give ourselves the
opportunity to be clothed in royal garments as heirs in the
kingdom of God, sharing in His royal dignity.

Formal Prayer

Formal prayer is vitally important to one's prayer life because
it takes prayer out of an intuitive state and places it into a
formal setting. Some examples of formal prayer are participating in daily Mass and praying the Rosary or the Chaplet
of Divine Mercy (much more on this later) or other daily
devotionals, such as reading from *The Imitation of Christ* or
meditating on the Seven Sorrows of Mary. Praying litanies
are also valuable formal prayers handed down through the

deposit of our Faith. Each of these activities require us to unplug from this world and draw ourselves towards God in a very specific and intentional way. It forces us to make time for God and use words and ideas that are not our own; hence, creating the opportunity for new life and connections to be made in us by the power and action of the Holy Spirit. It is also a form of humility, as we submit ourselves to ideas and prayers that are not our own and speak to God in ways which He has revealed to us through His Church over the centuries.

Many of our Protestant brethren will look down upon formal prayers such as the Rosary, Chaplet of Divine Mercy, and other formal devotions as simply a mindless repetition of words ("vain repetition"). But formal prayer is so much more because there is power in the words of God and in the Holy Names of Jesus, Mary, Joseph, the saints, the Blessed Sacrament, the Precious Blood, and others. Because Jesus's response to the apostles' request to "teach us how to pray" was to give them a formal prayer, it is reasonable to say that formal prayer is necessary and important. To this request, Jesus gave them a specific formula, which we know today as the Our Father, or Lord's Prayer. This prayer given to us by Jesus contains the seven perfect petitions,[9] all that one could ever want or need in a prayer. But the Church, in her wisdom and deep theological understanding, has developed additional forms of devotions and prayers to assist Christians in maintaining and growing their relationship with God.

---

[9] (1) Hallowed be Thy Name; (2) Thy Kingdom come; (3) Thy Will be done; (4) Give us this day our daily bread; (5) Forgive us our trespasses; (6) Lead us not into temptation; (7) Deliver us from evil.

Dedicating twenty to thirty minutes of formal prayer each day is a great foundation on which one can build. Though this may seem like a lot of time, it really is not. Daily Mass is about thirty minutes, a Rosary takes fifteen to twenty, and a Chaplet of Divine Mercy takes about seven. But for those just starting out, I would echo the advice of the all the great spiritual directors by recommending the Rosary to start. Of all the formal prayers, the Rosary is one of the greatest spiritual weapons in the Catholic arsenal, a sure way of growing in the Christian life. The Rosary has been present at every major turning point in Christian history since it was given to us. Because of its importance, there will be an entire chapter dedicated to the power of the Rosary towards the end of this book. There are some who think the Rosary is about the Blessed Virgin Mary, but when properly understood, it is clear that the Rosary is a dedicated time of meditation on twenty principle points in the life of Christ, taken directly from the Gospels. Therefore, it is a Christocentric prayer. When praying the Rosary, we sit with the Blessed Virgin Mary *and* Jesus to embark on a journey through the Gospels (we are always with Jesus if we are with His holy Mother!).

I have recommended the Rosary as one of the most powerful formal prayers in the Catholic arsenal. This is because for eight hundred years, the Rosary has aided in every major victory over evil. However, by the end of this book, I hope to show that of all the formal prayers at our disposal, next to the Mass, *the Divine Mercy Chaplet is the most powerful of all the formal prayers in our arsenal.* Yes, even more powerful than the Rosary, though of course we should pray both. Thus, the Chaplet of Divine Mercy will be of the greatest assistance in your spiritual battle and should be seen hand-in-hand with the Rosary in defeating all future evils.

Time in Scripture

Why should I make time for Sacred Scripture? Simply put, because it is the Word of God!

The Sacred Scriptures will assist in obtaining our eternal salvation and growth in the Christian life. Unfortunately, for Catholics, commitment and devotion to reading the Sacred Scriptures is often neglected or an afterthought. One of the greatest examples for why time spent reading Sacred Scripture is so important can be seen by looking to our faith-filled Protestant brothers and sisters. We all know non-Catholics who are exemplary Christians; some far superior in their love, knowledge, devotion, and service than most Catholics. They became this way through humility and by submitting themselves to the biblical principles found in the sacred text. They spend time and dive deeply into the Scriptures, seeking communion with God. They open their hearts to be discipled by the actions of the Holy Spirit through the words of the Sacred Scriptures. "For the word of God is living and active, sharper than any two-edged sword, piercing to the division of soul and spirit, of joints and marrow, and discerning the thoughts and intentions of the heart" (Heb 4:12).

During my personal conversion journey—going from agnostic to "spiritual," spiritual to Christian, and then ultimately Catholic—I visited a Bible church in Austin, Texas. My roommate attended this church and invited me, even though I was still undecided on my feelings toward Jesus Christ as God and religion as a whole. As the youth minister preached, towards the end of his sermon, he made the following challenge: "If you want to better your life forever, pick up the New Testament and read one chapter every day. Try it for two months. And if you doubt God's existence, start in the Gospel of John." I still remember how that challenge resonated in my soul. I thought to myself, "I will take this challenge, and when you're wrong, I can cross off Christianity from my list and be done with it forever." Reading a single chapter of the New Testament each day only takes about five minutes. So, I accepted the challenge. That evening when I got home, I dusted off an old Bible, given to me at my confirmation, and opened it up to John, chapter one, verse one.

Throughout my life, I struggled with severe learning disabilities from dyslexia to ADHD. Reading was a struggle and a chore. But reading the sacred text was surprisingly impactful. I found that it spoke with boldness and authority, like nothing I had read before. Each day over the next two months, I began to be immersed in the power of the Holy Spirit and began to encounter God through it. It was tremendously impactful, so much so that an impossible to ignore irony came out of all this: I owe this Bible church in Austin, Texas a debt of gratitude for assisting in my vocation to the Catholic priesthood. God works in mysterious ways!

Making a commitment to spend at least ten minutes a day reading the Bible is a great addition to your daily plan of prayer. There are various ways to accomplish your ten minutes with the Bible. It can be done as I just described, reading one chapter of the New Testament per day; you can read and meditate on the daily Mass readings (found at usccb.org); you can engage in a Bible study offered by so many great Catholic publishers, schools, and institutions, or you can develop your own approach to encountering the Scriptures. The point is not the exact number of minutes you spend doing this but rather that you have *intentionally* carved out time from your day for God to speak to you.

Silence

"But when you pray, go into your inner room, shut your door, and pray to your Father, who is unseen. And your Father, who sees what is done in secret, will reward you" (Mt 6:6).

Silence is absolutely necessary to hear the voice of God. There are countless examples throughout Sacred Scripture where God is heard or experienced in and from silence. God loves us and desires to give Himself to us, but, as it is said, God is a gentleman who will not barge in and interrupt your day. Instead, He invites us to Him whenever we are ready. He is most interested in meeting in the middle, where both parties are willing to give and receive of each other. We call this *communion*. Without making time for silence, we will miss the opportunity to encounter and hear the voice of God, and to perceive His inner promptings. You must learn how God speaks to your heart, and that can only be accomplished over time and in silence.

One of the greatest obstacles to obtaining silence these days is our technology. Whether it is the constant dinging of our smartphones or the hundred thousand impressions made on our minds throughout the day from surfing the internet or interacting in society, mankind lives in the noisiest environment in the history of the world. Though all of this noise may seem "natural," you can imagine how the devil will use this to his advantage for the destruction of souls. If he can keep us distracted, a person could go through life without ever hearing the voice of God. As a matriarch of a family once told me, "If the devil can't make you bad, he'll make you busy." The more noise in our lives, the busier our minds become.

To hear the voice of God, we must make space for silence every day. Because silence is so important to one's spiritual life, we should give God our time when we are at our best. Some of us are morning people, while others are at their best in the evening. It does not matter when you choose to do it, just do it! Start with ten to fifteen minutes each day and build from there. You can use that time to meditate on the Scripture you recently read (*lectio divina*) or just use that time to converse with God. Or, even better, *just be still* (see Ps 46:10). In his book *The Power of Silence: Against the Dictatorship of Noise*, Cardinal Sarah says, "Silence gives birth to silence." Times of silence start small, but if we are faithful to the practice, it will organically grow to the point where we will prefer the silence over the noise. This inevitably translates into loving God more than the world.

Continuing Education and Formation

You cannot expect a fire to grow larger or brighter unless you add new logs to it. Logs too small burn up instantly, and logs too big could smother it. You have to choose what works.

Part of developing our prayer life involves nourishing it with new information about our Faith. In our modern world, this is easily accomplished because the internet is filled with great Catholic resources. Whether it is watching short videos on YouTube or searching for a book on the life of a saint, any regular exposure to faithful Catholic content will help you grow your spiritual life.

Though I recommend daily exposure (+/- fifteen minutes) to some type of Catholic content, it is not necessary to do it every day. Rather, it is important to have it in your mind that you will have "regular" exposure to this content to support your spiritual life. For some, setting aside fifteen minutes every day works. For others, they might prefer spending forty-five to sixty minutes reading a spiritual book or watching long videos twice a week. Either way, the mind and the soul are being formed and nourished.

Monthly Plan for Receiving the Sacraments: Mass, Adoration, Confession

Going back to that notion of *if we cannot measure it, we cannot manage it,* it is helpful to have a plan for participating in the regular sacraments of our Faith, specifically Holy Mass and confession. Clearly, every Catholic's minimum goal is to attend Mass on Sunday, but can you do more? Is it possible to attend daily Mass sometime during the week? Making the effort to participate in a daily Mass is a tremendous way to nourish your spiritual life.[10]

---

[10] The website www.masstimes.org is fantastic for finding just about any church in the US and information about their Mass, adoration, and confession times.

When it comes to daily Mass attendance, there is an opportunity to purify our intention for going. Many people will say, "I love going to daily Mass and receiving Jesus in Holy Communion." This is a wonderful reason for going! However, a better way of approaching Sunday and daily Mass is to go into Mass with the mindset and intention of worshiping almighty God through the sacrifice of the Mass; I am here to give God my very best attention, all of my love and all of myself in this worship. And, by giving God the Father our very best, He will not be outdone in generosity but will then nourish us with His Son through Holy Communion. It is God Who invites us forward to receive Him.

The question for each of us is: What is a reasonable goal for daily Mass attendance? Maybe you could try to make daily Mass two of the four Saturdays each month, or pick up an early morning Mass or a 5:30 p.m. Mass each week before or after work. For those who live in the city, there are always opportunities to make it to the occasional daily Mass. The question is: What is your goal?

Now let us talk about adoration. If you love someone, you will want to spend time with that person. Around the country, there have been many churches that have expressed their love for Jesus by establishing perpetual adoration chapels. Here, anyone can step into the church or side chapel and sit with Jesus for a time. However, to spend time with Jesus's real presence, Eucharistic exposition or perpetual adoration is not necessary. Jesus is equally present behind the doors of the tabernacle as He is when enthroned in the monstrance. So, regardless of how you get to visit Jesus (in the monstrance or in the tabernacle), it is important for us to set a monthly goal to visit Jesus in the Blessed Sacrament. There are many reasons for this, but the main reason is because Jesus has made Himself the "prisoner of the tabernacle" for our sake, not His. In most churches, Jesus is abandoned, ignored, treated with contempt; these are not my words but the very words of Jesus Himself to Saint Margret Mary Alacoque in 1674. "Behold this heart which has so loved men as to spare Itself nothing, even to exhausting and consuming Itself, to testify to them Its love, and in return I receive nothing but ingratitude from the greater part of men by contempt, irreverence, sacrileges, and coldness which they have for Me in this Sacrament of My love; but what is still more painful is that it is hearts consecrated to Me that treat Me thus."[11]

Making time in your day to drop by your closest parish church and spend just five or ten minutes with Jesus on a regular basis will change your life. On top of this, Jesus will not be outdone in gratitude. If you have to make a sacrifice to visit Him, how much more will He give you in return?

And finally, confession. In order to receive Jesus in Holy Communion, we must be in a state of grace, meaning we have confessed any known mortal sins, received absolution, done our penance, and refrained from any mortal sins since then. The best practice is to examine ourselves daily and to go to confession regularly. It is good to strive to go to confession once per month, even if you are only confessing venial sins. Making a monthly confession is not about being scrupulous; it is about trusting in the power of the sacrament

---

[11] Jean Croiset, *Devotion to the Sacred Heart of Jesus: How to Practice the Sacred Heart Devotion* (Charlotte, NC: TAN Books, 2007), 59–60.

to heal your soul. Every time a person goes to confession and receives absolution, whether from venial or mortal sins, the soul receives extraordinary graces that flow directly from Calvary. Archbishop Fulton Sheen taught that when a priest traces the sign of the cross over the penitent to absolve him of his sins, it is the Precious Blood of Jesus that drips from the hand of the priest over the soul of the penitent. Said another way, when a person goes to confession and receives absolution, it is as if the priest's hand is like a scalpel that cuts through time and space, all the way back to the passion of Jesus Christ. As he makes the sign of the cross over the penitent, the graces of Calvary are applied to the individual's soul, and the soul is washed clean, healed, and strengthened. If the soul was dead in sin, it is now restored to life. This is the power of confession. This is the power of Divine Mercy.

Bodily/Corporeal Penance

Our Lady of Fatima appeared to the three shepherd children, telling them that multitudes of souls fall into hell like snowflakes because no one prays and offers sacrifices for them. One of the principal points of the message of Fatima was the necessity for physical penance and sacrifice. One does not need to scourge oneself each week, but there needs to be a mindset of self-sacrifice and self-denial. An easy way of doing this would be to give up unnecessary internet and entertainment for a day each week, or designate one day a week for cold or cool showers. Of course, we can always unite ourselves with Jesus through fasting, giving up a meal or things we like. When it comes to fasting from food, one must consider what is prudent, reasonable for your state in life, and safe for your health.

There are unlimited ways to take on reasonable forms of penance; the key is to plan for it and then actually do it! I like to recommend that, in addition to the customary penitential Friday, a person designates a particular weekday to make it his extra day of penance. If we are intentional in our planning, we are more likely to follow through. The question for you is: What can you do and what is your plan to carry it out?

A Plan for Service

In his book *Reflection on the Psalms*, C. S. Lewis points out that in the parable of the judgment of the nations (Mt 25:31–46), those who were condemned to hell were condemned not for what they did but for what they did not do: "Then they also will answer, 'Lord, when did we see thee hungry or thirsty or a stranger or naked or sick or in prison, and did not minister to thee?' Then he will answer them, 'Truly, I say to you, as you did it not to one of the least of these, you did it not to me.' And they will go away into eternal punishment, but the righteous into eternal life" (Mt 25:44–46).

Let us think back to the previous section on visiting Jesus in the Blessed Sacrament and how we said that He is often left alone in our churches, cold and hungry for our love. We can see a link to this passage in how our neighbors, in whom we should see Christ, are likewise left alone, cold, and hungry. Just as we must embrace adoration by visiting Jesus in the tabernacle or monstrance, we must also go our brothers and sisters in need.

The primary way we live out this commandment of service to others is through the Corporeal and Spiritual Works of Mercy. These are as follows:

The Spiritual Works of Mercy	The Corporal Works of Mercy
• Admonish the sinner.	• Feed the hungry.
• Instruct the ignorant.	• Give drink to the thirsty.
• Counsel the doubtful.	• Clothe the naked.
• Comfort the sorrowful.	• Visit the imprisoned.
• Bear wrongs patiently.	• Shelter the homeless.
• Forgive all injuries.	• Visit the sick.
• Pray for the living and the dead.	• Bury the dead.

All these actions kill the self-love that lives in our hearts by forcing us to go outside ourselves to serve others. Self-love is a weapon—arguably *the* weapon—the devil uses against us in spiritual warfare, so to deny him this weapon is incredibly advantageous to our success. Our prayer and sacramental life are of the utmost importance in the battle, but for this reason, so is service to others.

Live Your Faith, and Run Away!

Spiritual warfare is not about looking to pick a fight with the devil or fallen angels but being ready for the fight by simply living our Faith. What I have detailed in this chapter is not an exhaustive or exclusive "how to" when it comes to defeating the forces of darkness, but it is a good framework that will help create a foundation on which to build. The goal is to have a plan and intentionally live it every day, similar to how a general has a plan for battle and sees that it is carried out.

It is true that diabolic activity is real and the ordinary means of repelling their attacks are to stay in a state of grace, to sanctify your daily lives, and to properly use sacramentals. But the most active means of fighting the devil is to run away—that is, run to Jesus, Mary, Saint Joseph, Saint Michael, your guardian angel, and all the saints and angels. Run to your spiritual family if you find yourself under attack. Those who feel they can take on the devil on their own will be sorely mistaken. Let Mother Mary come to your assistance. Let Saint Michael fight for you (after all, he already once defeated Satan and one-third of the angels).[12] And let the power that flows from the Merciful Heart of Jesus come to your assistance.

---

[12] See Revelation 12.

CHAPTER 3

CONFESSION: A WEAPON IN THE BATTLE FOR SOULS

*"Many times, I have written that Satan is much more enraged
when we [priests] take souls away from him through confession
than when we take away bodies through exorcism."*[13]

—Fr. Gabriele Amorth

The Power of Confession

Fr. Gabriele Amorth served as an exorcist and then the chief
exorcist of Rome from 1986 until his death in 2016. For
thirty years, Father Amorth preformed over seventy thousand exorcisms. In many of his writings, interviews, and
books, he spoke of the immense power of the sacrament of
confession. In one interview, he explained that in some cases
of possession, a thorough sacramental confession is enough
to liberate a person from the control of the devil.

Listen to the words of Our Lord to Saint Faustina about
the power of confession:

---

[13] Gabriele Amorth, *An Exorcist Tells His Story* (San Francisco, CA: Ignatius Press, 1990), 67 (emphasis added).

Write, speak of My mercy. Tell souls where they are to look for solace; that is, in the Tribunal of Mercy [the confessional]. There the greatest miracles take place [and] are incessantly repeated. To avail oneself of this miracle, it is not necessary to go on a great pilgrimage or to carry out some external ceremony; it suffices to come with faith to the feet of My representative and to reveal to him one's misery, and the miracle of Divine Mercy will be fully demonstrated. Were a soul like a decaying corpse so that from a human standpoint, there would be no [hope of] restoration and everything would already be lost, it is not so with God. The miracle of Divine Mercy restores that soul in full. Oh, how miserable are those who do not take advantage of the miracle of God's mercy! You will call out in vain, but it will be too late. (*Diary* 1448)

Though we touched on the sacrament of confession in the last chapter, it merits a chapter of its own because it is one of the single greatest weapons against the diabolic. A sacramental confession frees the sinner from the hands of the devil and immerses him in the love of God. At every confession, the fullness of the graces of Christ's sacrifice on Calvary is poured out on each individual soul; it is as if Christ died for you, and you alone.

Satan, however, tempts us to deny responsibility for our sins, or even worse, presume that God is not offended by them. Our only defense is to take responsibility for our sins and throw ourselves at the feet of our merciful Savior. The only weapon that can defeat the prince of darkness is light; to overturn a kingdom ruled by pride, we need humility. Prior to your confession, you will need to examine your conscience. Even though you may be overtly aware of a grave sin that is prominent in your life, it is worthwhile to read through an examination of conscience pamphlet to see what else might be associated with that sin, or what other areas you have been failing in.[14]

The Spiritual Effects of a Good Confession

The *Catechism of the Catholic Church* (*CCC* 1496) tells us the spiritual effects of a good confession:

- Reconciliation with God by which the penitent recovers grace
- Reconciliation with the Church
- Remission of the eternal punishment incurred by mortal sins
- Remission, at least in part, of temporal punishments resulting from sin
- Peace and serenity of conscience, and spiritual consolation
- An increase of spiritual strength for the Christian battle

Confession requires repentance, or sorrow for sin, resolve to change, and the commitment to avoid the near occasion of

---

[14] In the back of this book, you will find a thorough examination of conscience published by the Fathers of Mercy; you can also download a free copy of this same examination by going to our website at www. fathersofmercy.com.

sin. This is why Saint John Chrysostom once said, "Leading a person to a moral conversion is a greater miracle than raising a person from the dead." What does he mean by this? To raise a person from the dead is, in a sense, really not that difficult. All one must do is ask God to do it. If it is God's will, God will send the soul back into the body of the deceased, heal what lead to death in the first place, and turn everything "back on." However, a moral conversion requires one with courage to speak the truth and one with humility to receive it. In addition, there is the spiritual battle going on, meaning the diabolic is working overtime to disrupt the reception of the truth. Though this is an oversimplification of both processes, it gives us a broad understanding of how much more complex is moral conversion.

Here are several quotes emphasizing the importance of conversion and repentance:

> Just so, I tell you, there will be more joy in heaven over one sinner who repents than over ninety-nine righteous persons who need no repentance. (Lk 15:7)

> Christ instituted the sacrament of Penance for all sinful members of his Church: above all for those who, since Baptism, have fallen into grave sin, and have thus lost their baptismal grace and wounded ecclesial communion. It is to them that the sacrament of Penance offers a new possibility to convert and to recover the grace of justification. The Fathers of the Church present this sacrament as "the second plank [of salvation] after the shipwreck which is the loss of grace. (*CCC* 1446)

Today the Lord said to me, **Daughter, when you go to confession, to this fountain of My mercy, the Blood and Water which came forth from My Heart always flows down upon your soul and ennobles it. Every time you go to confession, immerse yourself in My mercy, with great trust, so that I may pour the bounty of My grace upon your soul. When you approach the confessional, know this, that I Myself am waiting there for you. I am only hidden by the priest, but I myself act in your soul. Here the misery of the soul meets the God of mercy. Tell souls that from this fount of mercy souls draw graces solely with the vessel of trust. If their trust is great, there is no limit to My generosity. The torrents of grace inundate humble souls. The proud remain always in poverty and misery, because My grace turns away from them to humble souls.** (*Diary* 1602)

Faustina on Confession

Saint Faustina gives us three points of direction as it pertains to making a good confession:

I would like to say three words to the soul that is determined to strive for sanctity and to derive fruit; that is to say, benefit from confession.

First word – complete sincerity and openness. Even the holiest and wisest confessor cannot forcibly pour into the soul what he desires if it is not sincere and open. An insincere, secretive soul risks great dangers in the spiritual life, and even the Lord Jesus Himself does not give Himself to such a soul on a higher level, because He knows it would derive no benefit from these special graces.

Second word – humility. A soul does not benefit as it should from the sacrament of confession if it is not humble. Pride keeps it in darkness. The soul neither knows how, nor is willing, to probe the depths of its own misery. It puts on a mask and avoids everything that might bring it recovery.

Third word – obedience. A disobedient soul will win no victory, even if the Lord Jesus Himself, in person, were to hear its confession. (*Diary* 113)

Confession requires honesty, humility, and the desire to obey the teachings of Jesus Christ as it pertains to your state in life. When you come to confession, tell the priest all of your sins, with none of the stories, none of the justifications. *Simply confess, confess simply.* Many times, when a person begins to tell the background information related to the sin that was committed, there is an attempt to justify the sin in his own mind, which sets himself up for a repeat fall in that same area. To make a good confession, one simply needs to make a good examination of conscience. If necessary, make a list of your sins, then come to the sacrament and reveal your failings. If the priest needs more information, he will ask clarifying questions. In speaking of the role of the priest, hear the words of Jesus to Faustina: **"My daughter, just as you prepare in My presence, so also you make your confession before Me. The person of the priest is, for Me, only a screen. Never analyze what sort of a priest it is that I am**

making use of; open your soul in confession as you would to Me, and I will fill it with My light" (*Diary* 1725).

Confessing without Fear

It is important to never conceal (or willfully not confess) any of your sins to a priest; this would be a "bad confession," more technically called an invalid confession. Sometimes people are embarrassed by their sins and are afraid the priest will recognize their voice or think less of them. The reality is that priests are normally hearing one confession after another and almost never remember anything. (We call it confessor's brain). It is important to know that a confessor never thinks less of a person making his or her confession. Rather, we hold penitents in the highest esteem because they know they did wrong, have owned this reality, and are coming to Jesus to say sorry and ask for the grace to be better. Oh, that the whole world would go to confession! Parents, what would you think if your teenagers came up to you and said, "Mom, Dad, I need to tell you some things. Here are all the things I am doing wrong; I am really sorry for them and I want to be better." What would a good parent's response be?

In addition, a priest can never take what is said in the confession out from under the seal of confession. Even if the person comes up to the priest immediately after his or her confession and starts making references to what was said in the confessional, the priest cannot act on any knowledge obtained from a confession. If he willfully does, that priest immediately incurs excommunication.

We must confess without fear, because it is the merciful Jesus who waits for us there. Listen again to what He tells Faustina, followed by her own words:

> **Do not put off the Sacrament of Penance, because this displeases Me.**
>
> . . . I now understand the Lord's warning. I decided to call any priest at all, the next day, and to open the secrets of my soul to him . . . for while I was praying for sinners and offering all my sufferings for them, the Evil spirit could not stand that. (*Diary* 1464)

Our Lord's words invite us to a regular confession. As you go through your days and recognize the sins accumulating or feel the prompting to confess, go at the first opportunity you can find, because God wants to heal you and free you. In the event that you fall into mortal sin, do not wait! Treat it like an emergency and get to confession within the week. Your eternal salvation is at risk!

A Sacrament for Warfare

Confession is one of the greatest and most powerful resources we have in fighting the evil one. This is because it frees us from his grasp, heals the inner wounds that cause us to sin, fills us with sanctifying grace, and strengthens us for the battle. Confession is the field hospital for the soul; it puts us back together so we can get back in the fight!

This chapter is not just about us; it is about our family and friends as well. We should never hesitate to invite others to go with us to confession with us, especially if we know or suspect they have not been in quite some time. Back when I was in business, a report was circulating that the number one reason people did not buy a specific product was because they were not asked to do so. So, whether you are a priest, religious, or part of the laity, we should strive to create a culture of encouraging confession. Think how many souls go to hell because of lazy unrepentance. We have the opportunity to liberate souls from Satan's grasp just by inviting them to go to confession. We can share these examinations with them, but most importantly pray, fast, and do penance for the conversion of poor sinners. This is what God expects of us.

We touched on Faustina's diary in this chapter, zeroing in on the sacrament of confession. In our next chapter, though, we will highlight parts of the diary that deal specifically with spiritual warfare so that we can discover the treasures and weapons that are at our disposal through the Divine Mercy.

PART II

CALLING UPON THE DIVINE MERCY IN BATTLE

CHAPTER 4

THE IMAGE

A Devotion Like No Other

Over the next three chapters, we will be talking about the Divine Mercy image, Divine Mercy Sunday, and the Divine Mercy Chaplet, each as they pertain to engaging in spiritual warfare. As bold a claim as it may be, I would like to present these elements of the Divine Mercy not as one devotion among many but rather as gifts from God that carry with them greater power and efficaciousness than any other devotion in the life of the Church. More than that, I want us to share in the mentality of Saint John Paul II, who "sees [the Divine Mercy message] as more than just a collection of 'private revelations'"; rather, he sees them as "prophetic revelations."[15] When we approach these elements of the Divine Mercy message as having a prophetic dimension, as opposed to a purely devotional one, we will begin to experience for ourselves the power and fruitfulness associated with the power of a prophet.

There is much theological support for what I will be presenting and I do not want anyone to miss out on the gifts

---

[15] Robert Stackpole, "Understanding Divine Mercy," TheDivineMercy. org and John Paul II Institute of Divine Mercy, 2003, www.the divinemercy.org/assets/pdf/jpii/UnderstandDM.pdf.

that Jesus Christ wishes to give us. In addition, I think it is reasonable to approach these practices with greater faith and expectation because of the times we live in. These are the most turbulent and sinful times in world history, and *where sin abounds, grace abounds all the more* (see Rom 5:20). God has also warned us that this message of Divine Mercy is a message for the end times. These are not my words but the words of Jesus Christ Himself. **"Let all mankind recognize My unfathomable mercy. It is a sign for the end times; after it will come the day of justice"** (*Diary* 848). And again, **"You will prepare the world for My final coming"** (*Diary* 429). As sin continues to increase in number and kind, it makes sense that God would give us these extraordinary graces; the closer we get to the second coming of Jesus Christ, the greater and more powerful the gifts of God will be to save souls for the kingdom of heaven. Let us talk first of the wonderful gift of the Divine Mercy image.

The Sacred Heart Devotion and the Divine Mercy

One of the early challenges of the promulgation of the Divine Mercy devotion was the initial concern that it was in conflict (or even opposition) with the devotion to the Sacred Heart of Jesus, given by Jesus to Saint Margret Mary Alacoque. It appears that the root of the conflict was the concern that the Divine Mercy message would detract or take away from the message of reparation, the First Friday devotions, and promises associated with the Sacred Heart of Jesus. Looking back, historically, I get the sense that opponents of the Divine Mercy movement did not see how Divine Mercy is in communion with the Sacred Heart revelations given to Saint Margret Mary. So let's take a moment to refresh our memory on the events surrounding the Sacred Heart of Jesus.

Briefly, around 1673 to 1675, Mary Margaret, a simple French nun, was visited by Jesus and given a variety of messages and requests. At the heart of the messages was how grieved Jesus is by the treatment He (in the Blessed Sacrament) receives from "the better part of [humanity]." Here are His exact words: "Behold this heart which has so loved men as to spare Itself nothing, even to exhausting and consuming Itself, to testify to them Its love, and in return I receive nothing but ingratitude from the greater part of men by contempt, irreverence, sacrileges, and coldness which they have for Me in this Sacrament of My love; but what is still more painful is that it is hearts consecrated to Me that treat Me thus."[16]

Jesus went on to command that a feast day be established honoring His Sacred Heart (the first Friday after Corpus Christi). In addition to this day set aside to honor His Sacred Heart, there are other practices of the devotion, including observing "nine first Fridays" (attending Mass on the first Friday of each month for nine consecutive Fridays), that "love be returned for Love," and finally, that mankind perform penance for the way He has been treated. I emphasize the *love for Love* part because that is, explicitly, the most important element of this devotion: to love Jesus in return for the Love that He has given us. The principal element of this devotion

---

[16] Jean Croiset, *Devotion to the Sacred Heart of Jesus: How to Practice the Sacred Heart Devotion* (Charlotte, NC: TAN Books, 2007), 59–60.

is to love Jesus in the Blessed Sacrament, then offer various forms of penance in reparation for the sins committed against His Most Sacred Heart. One other aspect of His messages to Saint Margret Mary that often gets forgotten is that He told her mankind must "do this before it is too late."

Once vetted and approved by the Church, the devotion to the Sacred Heart of Jesus took the Universal Church and the world by storm, especially in France, with churches being built in its honor, devotions being kept, and Jesus's requests being fulfilled. Archbishop Fulton Sheen tells the story of going to the Basilica of Sacré-Cœur in Paris, France, where over one thousand men would be adoring Jesus in the Blessed Sacrament from 10 p.m. until the conclusion with Mass at 7 a.m. the next day. But despite the extraordinary warnings given to us by Jesus Himself, mankind's love and devotion began to fail. Devotions became more about the external behavior than the interior dispositions. Hearts began to grow cold and love waned.

As *love grew cold,* Our Lord decided to give mankind one last extraordinary opportunity to turn to Him. In 1932, he appeared to yet another simple and illiterate sister, Maria Faustina Kowalska. Sr. Faustina was a sister with the Congregation of the Sisters of Our Lady of Mercy in Warsaw. After approximately seven years into her religious vocation, she began receiving visions of and messages from Jesus to share with mankind. The following passage speaks of the beginning of her revelations:

> In the evening, when I was in my cell, I saw the Lord
> Jesus clothed in a white garment. One hand [was]

raised in the gesture of blessing, the other was touching the garment at the breast. From beneath the garment, slightly drawn aside at the breast, there were emanating two large rays, one red, the other pale. In silence I kept my gaze fixed on the Lord; my soul was struck with awe, but also with great joy. After a while, Jesus said to me, **Paint an image according to the pattern you see, with the signature: Jesus, I trust in You. I desire that this image be venerated, first in your chapel, and [then] throughout the world. I promise that the soul that will venerate this image will not perish. I also promise victory over [its] enemies already here on earth, especially at the hour of death. I Myself will defend it as My own glory.** (*Diary* 47–48)

As we can see, the first message to Saint Faustina was in relation to the image itself, but immediately after making this request, Jesus follows up with three inconceivable promises. We will revisit those promises in a moment, but let us finish with the comparison to the devotion to the Sacred Heart of Jesus.

Scholars and theologians will point out that there is absolutely no conflict between the two devotions, but rather much complementarity. First, when you compare the two images, you will notice that the hand positioning is almost identical, and as you study the messages, you will find key distinctions that make each their own message for mankind.

The devotion to the Divine Mercy highlights the Mercy of God in the Holy Trinity, while the devotion to the Sacred Heart of Jesus centers on the Son of God, specifically in the Blessed

Sacrament. The material subject of the devotion to the Divine Mercy is the image of the merciful Jesus, the vision Faustina was given; the devotion to the Sacred Heart, meanwhile, corresponds to the physical human heart of Jesus as revealed to Saint Margret Mary. The essential nature of the devotion to the Divine Mercy is a spirit of trust and conversion, while the devotion to the Sacred Heart is directly related to reparation.[17]

There are volumes of theological discourse that thoroughly address the distinctions between the two devotions. It is also reasonable to believe that practicing one of these devotions will make you better at the other. For me, it was the devotion to the Sacred Heart of Jesus that ultimately led me from agnosticism back to the Catholic Church (that is a story for another time). But having studied, and practiced, both devotions at great length, it is sufficient to say that both of these will lead you in to the depths of divine intimacy and growth in the spiritual life.

When speaking on how the Divine Mercy message is the fulfillment, or continuation, of the message of the Sacred Heart of Jesus, I simply summarize each devotion into a simple statement.

- In the messages of the Sacred Heart, Jesus essentially says, I grow weary of being maltreated; return love for love, then do penance, before it is to late!
- In the messages of the Divine Mercy, Jesus essentially says, *It's too late.* "Before the Day of Justice I am sending the Day of Mercy" (*Diary* 1588).

---

[17] Robert Stackpole, "The Difference Is in the Emphasis," *The Divine Mercy*, 5 Sept. 2019, https://www.thedivinemercy.org/articles/difference-emphasis.

We can easily observe how faith has waned and is even failing on an international scale. There are only a few places in the world where Catholicism is growing; most are in states of attrition. The pious practice of stopping by a local church for a few minutes each day has been forgotten and disregarded. This has resulted in the abandonment of Jesus in the Eucharist in most churches worldwide; even worse than the neglect are the sacrilegious communions that happen every Sunday.

A sacrilegious communion is the receiving of Jesus while in the known state of mortal sin or the willful mistreatment of Jesus in Holy Communion. Few Catholics go to confession on a regular basis, but almost everyone receives Holy Communion at Mass. To fall into mortal sin is easy, as easy as missing Mass on Sunday (or holy days of obligation) out of laziness or negligence, or willfully participating in sexual sins, such as pornography, fornication, adultery, sexual impurity with oneself, contraception or sterilization in marriage, remarriage without an annulment, marriage outside of the Church, or any number of other sins so commonplace today. Please examine yourself using the Fathers of Mercy examination of conscience or another one. Be certain you are in a state of grace prior to Eucharistic reception. We must be in a state of grace in order to receive Holy Communion or Saint Paul says there are consequences: "Whoever, therefore, eats the bread or drinks the cup of the Lord in an unworthy manner *will be guilty of profaning the body and blood of the Lord.* Let a man examine himself, and so eat of the bread and drink of the cup. For anyone who eats and drinks without discerning the body eats and drinks judgment upon himself.

That is why many of you are weak and ill, and some have died" (1 Cor 11:27–30, emphasis added).

As Our Lord indicated to Saint Margaret Mary, He has "exhausted" Himself in putting up with mistreatment. The Catholic world's relapse into indifferentism and the secular world's unrepentance and obstinance paints a very dire picture. One that only can be resolved by God's Divine Mercy.

Through the Divine Mercy, God is giving mankind one last opportunity to turn back to Him. If we go back to my summation of the two devotions—SHJ: *return love for love and do penance before it's too late*; DM: *It's too late*—we might think of it like a retail shop going out of business. When a store announces its closing, they will offer an initial sale of, say, 20 percent off everything, then 40 percent, then 80 percent, then in the final days, there will be a sign posted saying, "No reasonable offer will be refused!" This is what I hear Our Lord crying out to humanity, saying, "Just turn to me! Ask for My Mercy and I will give it!" Hence, the extraordinary graces that come from the Divine Mercy devotion.

You may be wondering how all this relates specifically to spiritual warfare. We will discover the answer to that next by turning to the Divine Mercy image.

The Image for War

When we look at the promises associated with the Divine Mercy image, we see these extraordinary graces at work. In the initial revelation of the image to Saint Faustina, we find three incredible promises (emphasis added):

1. I promise that the soul that will venerate this image *will not perish*.
2. I also *promise victory* over [its] enemies already here on earth, especially at the hour of death.
3. I Myself *will defend* [the soul] as My own glory.

The spiritual warfare imagery is impossible to ignore. Jesus tells us there is hardly a greater weapon than the veneration of the Divine Mercy image. To venerate simply means honoring or showing great respect to the representation of Jesus Christ in this image. As a person shows Christ this great honor and respect, Jesus, through an outpouring of grace, will then edify, instruct, and enliven the hearts of those who spend time with this image. The key is to venerate the image by spending time with it and by making acts of honor and reverence towards Christ in it. How much time? It can be a simple moment where you kiss a holy card or make the sign of the cross as you pass by the image, or you can also sit before the image for an extended period of time and meditate on it. Any attention you give Jesus through this image counts as veneration.

If you, or a person you know, feels under attack, overwhelmed, or constantly persecuted, spend time in front of the Divine Mercy image each day. Distribute it to believers and non-believers alike; encourage them to say the prayer at the bottom of the image: "Jesus, I trust in you." Then watch God fight for you and defend you!

Three additional references in Faustina's diary relate to the grace of the image:

I am offering people a vessel with which they are to keep coming for graces to the fountain of mercy. That vessel is this image with the signature: "Jesus, I trust in You." (*Diary* 327)

By means of this Image, I shall be granting many graces to souls; so, let every soul have access to it. (*Diary* 570)

Let the rays of grace enter your soul; they bring with them light, warmth, and life. (*Diary* 1486)

From a historical perspective, when Christians have made reference to the "fountain of mercy," it has typically been ascribed to the graces associated with the blood and water that flowed from the heart of Jesus when the centurion pierced His side as He hung upon the cross. Because Holy Mass is the re-presentation of the one perfect sacrifice of Jesus Christ on the cross, the Eucharist has also been referred to as the "fountain of mercy." So, the blood and water continue to gush forth from the side of Christ in the Eucharist, not in a literal but in a mystical sense. "[In the Mass,] the same Christ who offered himself once in a bloody manner on the altar of the cross is contained and offered in an unbloody manner" (*CCC* 1367). By extension, as we read in the diary passage 327, Jesus is offering us access to the fullness of the graces that flow from the Eucharist, from the Mass, from Calvary through this holy image!

The Divine Mercy image acts as an icon or window that connects the one venerating it to the graces associated with the blood and water that flow from the side of Jesus Christ. The two rays are distinctive features in the image. When asked to explain them, Jesus responded, **"The pale ray stands for the Water which makes souls righteous. The red ray stands for the Blood which is the life of souls. . . . Happy is the one who will dwell in their shelter"** (*Diary* 299). Thus, we find in these rays an allusion to the sacraments of Baptism and Penance, which purify the soul, and the Eucharist, which nourishes it.

We can see then that sitting before the image of Divine Mercy is not a passive activity; you can trust that when you put yourself in its presence, Jesus is working on you. "Let the rays of grace enter your soul," He tells us. There may be times where there is a perceptible experience from spending time in the presence of the image, while other times there may not be; but regardless, trust in the promises Jesus has made to you. Let the purifying ray purify, and the nourishing ray nourish.

So please, dear reader, use this image as an offensive weapon in the battle for your soul. Let Christ come to your aide. For yourself and for those you love, even those you may barely know, obtain a beautiful copy of the Divine Mercy image and have it blessed and framed. If you are giving it away, gift wrap it and present it to those people in your lives who are struggling with faith. Some will receive it with great appreciation, others may not. But rest assured, grace will begin to flow into their souls.

I remember our vice rector told us one year in seminary about a family he met and had helped through some difficult times. Father would visit this family maybe twice a year. After a few years, the children began to grow closer to and get familiar with his visits. One year, the six-year-old comes to him and says, "Father, Father, I knew you were coming, I just knew it. I always know when you are coming."

"How is it that?" he asked.

"Because the statue of Jesus comes out of storage!"

Now, maybe you spend time and money giving a grace-filled spiritual gift to people, and maybe those gifts end up in storage. Regardless of where they end up, they are still in these people's homes, with the graces of Calvary flowing through them, flooding the house with the peace of Jesus Christ, present to disrupt diabolic activities. Can you imagine the joy of the guardian angles watching over those in these homes and how much more effective they might be from the divine assistance given through the image? And maybe one day—just maybe—the recipient will be near that image and make some type of response to the constant torrent of grace poured forth from it. Think of the individual that might just stop in front of it in a time of distress and ask for Jesus's help. Or think about your grandchildren, who will be living and playing in Jesus's presence, and those graces that may be affecting them. This type of action is not superstition; it is an act of faith.

Let me close with another story. I remember hearing of a child who helped lead her family into a deeper conversion. This family had a crucifix in an entryway of the home. One day, they found their youngest daughter, maybe four or five years old, standing beneath the cross, singing, "Twinkle, Twinkle, Little Star." The mother came around the corner to investigate and asked the little one what she was doing. The child responded, "I heard that Jesus was all alone on the cross, so I wanted to keep Him company." How wonderful is the faith and innocence of a child! Just imagine how Jesus will come to the defense of this little girl later in life when she is attacked by the devil. Let us, too, keep Jesus company; let us love Him and console Him so that when our time for battle comes, He will be by our side.

With our examination of the Divine Mercy image complete, let us move on now to discuss the feast of Divine Mercy, another channel of grace Holy Mother Church provides us during these troubled times.

CHAPTER 5

THE FEAST

Healing before Battle

An often-neglected aspect of spiritual warfare is the restoration, or healing, of an individual. Life is difficult, full of sinfulness and failures. If we want to fight for our souls, we must be healed from this brokenness, this woundedness, this sinfulness, just as a soldier cannot march into battle if he is wounded. This restoration is not only important for ourselves but for our neighbor too, as we accompany our fellow soldiers in their own battles.

The normative way of healing is through the sacrament of confession, where Jesus says, **"Here the greatest miracles take place [and] are incessantly repeated"** (*Diary* 1488). Even so, there is a single day each year for even greater graces, greater healing, and greater liberation. That day is Divine Mercy Sunday.

Our Lord tells us that on Divine Mercy Sunday, the soul who has gone (or will go) to confession (within twenty days) and receives Holy Communion in a state of grace will receive the total renewal of their baptismal graces (see *Diary* 699). They will receive the total and complete healing of their soul and the total forgiveness of *all* temporal punishment due to sin. Unlike a plenary indulgence, there are *no other* actions or dispositions necessary to receive this extraordinary grace. Also, unlike a plenary indulgence, the fruits of this meritorious act are for the individual alone and cannot be offered for another.

The Unique Power of This Feast

Normally when I preach (or write) on the feast of Divine Mercy Sunday, I like to build up this teaching and present it dramatically as a "great reveal." However, in my travels, I have encountered two big issues: (1) There are many faithful parishes or dioceses that mistakenly claim that this promise of Jesus for Divine Mercy Sunday only equates to a plenary indulgence, and (2) people are totally unaware that these promises and graces exist.

In this book, I do not want to leave any room for confusion. Rather, let us come straight to the point, which is that on Divine Mercy Sunday, the soul who meets those two conditions (confession and communion) will receive *the total renewal of its baptismal graces.*

This teaching comes directly from Our Lord Himself:

> **Whoever approaches the Fount of Life on this day will be granted complete remission of sins and punishment.** (*Diary* 300)

> **I desire that the Feast of Mercy be a refuge and shelter for all souls, and especially for poor sinners. On that day the very depths of My tender mercy are open. I pour out a whole ocean of graces upon those souls who approach the Fount of My Mercy.**

> **The soul that will go to Confession and receive Holy Communion shall obtain complete forgiveness of sins and punishment. On that day all the divine floodgates through which graces flow are opened. Let no soul fear to draw near to Me, even though its sins be as scarlet. My mercy is so great that no mind, be it of man or of angel, will be able to fathom it throughout all eternity.** (*Diary* 699)

> **I want to grant a complete pardon to the souls that will go to Confession and receive Holy Communion on the Feast of My mercy.** (*Diary* 1109)

The questions related to this extraordinary grace, of the *renewal of baptismal graces,* prompted a full review of the issue, and a theological response was compiled. In 2003, the John Paul II Institute of Divine Mercy published a forty-page document entitled "Understanding Divine Mercy Sunday." This document, that carries with it an Imprimi Potest and Nihil Obstat, walks us through the theological validity of such extraordinary graces.

While it is good for the Church to rely on the studies of theologians, the average Catholic need only listen to the words of Jesus. He literally says, "The soul that will go to Confession and receive Holy Communion *shall obtain complete forgiveness* of sins and punishment." In the sentence prior, He says, "On that day . . . *I pour out a whole ocean of graces* upon those souls who approach the Fount of My Mercy." Jesus then goes on to say, "On that day *all the divine floodgates* through which graces flow are opened. Let no soul fear to draw near to Me, even though its sins be as scarlet.

My mercy is so great that *no mind, be it of man or of angel, will be able to fathom it throughout all eternity.*" This does not sound like any ordinary day or set of graces! This last statement shows us that something so much greater than a regular plenary indulgence is at work. With this being true, let every priest proclaim from the pulpit, let every faithful voice proclaim this from the rooftops (or every social media platform) that these graces are available! Can you imagine what would happen if, worldwide, every parish for the three weeks prior to Divine Mercy Sunday offered confessions and truly prepared their people for Holy Week and Easter, but also for this very special grace to be received the following Sunday? This would literally change the course of world events. I do not know that heaven itself could contain the joy of such a response.

As a revert to the Catholic faith, and a man who was once a very difficult prodigal son, I found myself a little jealous of a friend of mine who converted to Catholicism and was baptized in his forties. That meant his original sin, all his personal sins, and all temporal punishment due to sin was wiped away. If my friend would have died at that moment, he would have gone straight to heaven without any concern for purgatory. Through the graces conferred at Baptism, his entire sinful past was annihilated by the grace of his sacramental baptism. In short, he had no debt of sin, while I had a lifetime of debt. Of course, this is all before I understood the graces associated with Divine Mercy Sunday!

A Hostage Rescue

Coming back to our theme of spiritual warfare, we can see how horribly the devil is beat down on Divine Mercy Sunday as souls hemorrhage from his grasp. Every soul that participates according to Jesus's wishes is fully healed and restored (the total renewal of their baptismal graces). There are stories of sinners who experienced amazing conversions from even participating somewhat casually in this invitation, going from cold or lukewarm to blazing hot for Jesus and His Church. As a confessor, I can testify to the words of Jesus, who said the "greatest miracles happen in the confessional."

Going forward, we are all commissioned to work towards a *hostage rescue* every year, not only to restore and heal those who are faithful, but explicitly to invite those who have fallen away to come back home, those who are held captive by the enemy. When one of our brothers or sisters is imprisoned, we of course want to free them. However, we must not go in haphazardly; we must do so at the right time. That time is Divine Mercy Sunday. That is the time we must make our move into enemy territory in search of captives.

We all know people in our lives who have fallen away from the practice of their Catholic faith and have not been to confession in years. Make it a point to reach out to them and invite them to come home. Print out the free examination from the Fathers of Mercy and pass that out to friends and family. Do everything you can to help bring home a prodigal son or daughter!

Turning from sin, and helping others to do so, is a great form of spiritual warfare. It has been said that the easiest way of casting out the darkness is to make the fire burn brighter. One candle burns brightly, but place two or three in proximity of each other and allow their flames to touch, and you have instant exponential growth from a flame to a fire. Jesus said, "I have come to set the earth on fire, and how I wish it were already blazing!" (Lk 12:49). Let us help set the stage for this new holy fire by our own personal conversions first, then by the invitation to others.

In our next chapter, we will reveal a powerful weapon the Divine Mercy devotion offers us to free our brothers and sisters, and to protect ourselves. We will talk about the Divine Mercy Chaplet.

CHAPTER 6

THE CHAPLET

The Most Powerful Weapon

When going into battle, a warrior must have the greatest armor and the most effective weapons to accomplish his ends. The same principle applies to each of us engaging in this spiritual war. We want to be protected, but also to be able to attack with swift and decisive blows to subdue the wicked foe. Remember Jesus's words to Saint Faustina, **"Fight like a knight"** (*Diary* 1760). Of all the devotional weapons in our arsenal, I would like to suggest that the Divine Mercy Chaplet is the greatest of them, even more powerful than the Rosary.

The claim that the Chaplet is more powerful than the Rosary is *not* for the sake of pitting one devotion against the other, but for the sake of increasing your faith in both devotions. The last thing I want to see is a person putting down the mysteries of the Rosary and devotion to our Blessed Mother. Rather, I want to encourage the faithful to *add* the Chaplet to your daily arsenal of prayer. The Rosary was given to Saint Dominc in the 1200s and has proven, around every major world crisis, that our heavenly Mother's intercession is beyond compare. However, with that said, I posit that the Chaplet of Divine Mercy has greater power because it unites the one praying to Jesus's perfect sacrifice on Calvary and thus can be considered a direct extension of the Liturgy of the Eucharist of the Mass (specifically, the Great Doxology: "Through him, and with him, and in him, O God, almighty Father, in the unity of the Holy Spirit, all glory and honor is yours, for ever and ever. Amen."). When we pray the Chaplet, we find ourselves not only united to Jesus's perfect sacrifice but also united with the Blessed Virgin Mary, who stood at the foot of the cross (see Jn 19:25).

The Sacred Mass and the Chaplet

As indicated previously, the Mass is the mystical link to the sacrifice on Calvary; so, by extension, the Chaplet connects us with the same event and graces. Said another way, the same graces that flowed on Calvary flow through the Mass and, yes, the Chaplet.

This mystical connection is discovered when we examine and question the prayers of the Chaplet of Divine Mercy.[18] The primary prayer, prayed on the rosary beads where the Our Father is normally said, reads:

> **Eternal Father, I offer you the Body and Blood, Soul and Divinity of Your Dearly Beloved Son, Our Lord, Jesus Christ, in atonement for our sins and those of the whole world.**

Then, ten times on the beads where one would pray the Hail Mary, we say:

---

[18] The Divine Mercy Chaplet is prayed using rosary beads. If you are unfamiliar with the Rosary, please research it online and learn how to pray this powerful prayer. We will be referencing the Rosary as we teach the Divine Mercy Chaplet.

For the sake of His sorrowful Passion, have mercy on us and on the whole world.

The parallels between the words of the Chaplet and what happens at Mass are identical. As noted previously, the majority of the prayers at Mass are directed to God the Father. The heart of the Mass is the sacrificial offering of the Son to the Father.

When teaching on how to fight distractions during Mass, I advise people to be attentive to who you are speaking to, who is doing the speaking, and what are you saying/doing in that moment. The three points present reveal themselves when we break down the main prayer of the Chaplet of Divine Mercy:

Who is speaking?	"I" – the individual who is praying
Who am I speaking to?	The "Eternal Father"
What are you doing?	Offering
What are you offering?	The Body, Blood, Soul, and Divinity of Jesus Christ
For what reason?	For the atonement of our sins and those of the whole world

When we worship at Mass, we are present with the Blessed Virgin Mary, Saint John, Mary Magdalene, and the other Mary, who are at the foot of the cross, joining themselves to Jesus's sacrifice and interceding for all of humanity. When we pray the Chaplet of Divine Mercy, *we are entering into that same mystical action*: offering to God the Father Jesus Christ crucified, in sorrow for our sins, begging Him for the conversion of sinners. When we pray the Chaplet of Divine Mercy, we are entering into the mystical realities of the Mass as depicted in book of Revelation.[19]

Breaking this down further, we see how intimately this prayer is connected to the Mass. In the Chaplet, the individual participates in the action of "offering" the "Body, Blood, Soul, and Divinity of Jesus Christ." Where do we find the Body, Blood, Soul, and Divinity of Jesus Christ? In the Most Blessed Sacrament, made present through the hands of the ministerial priest at every Mass. The *Catechism of the Catholic Church* teaches that "at the moment of consecration" (*CCC* 1377), the bread and wine "become Christ's body and blood" (*CCC* 1333). "The body and blood, together with the soul and divinity, of our Lord Jesus Christ and, therefore, the whole Christ is truly, really, and substantially contained" (*CCC* 1374). The action of the bread and wine changing into Jesus's substantial presence is referred to as transubstantiation (*CCC* 1376).

The challenge with the main prayer of the Chaplet is that it says, "Eternal Father, *I* offer you . . ." Catholics are aware that it is only the ministerial priest who can make the Eucharist present at Mass. As the old saying goes, "No priest, No Eucharist." So, how is it possible for the lay faithful to "offer" the Eternal Father, the Body, Blood, Soul, and Divinity of Jesus when that is reserved to the ministerial priest?

---

[19] See Scott Hahn, *The Lamb's Supper: The Mass as Heaven on Earth* (New York: Double Day, 1999).

The answer lies in the Vatican II document "The Constitution on the Sacred Liturgy" (*CSL - Sacrosanctum Concilium*). In this document, the Church gives us the term "active participation" in relation to the laity's role in the sacred liturgy. Unfortunately, this term has been one of the most abused and misunderstood terms in the post-Vatican II era. For many, active participation meant that more people from the laity needed to "do" [actions] in the Mass and liturgy. However, when one reads the document, it is clear that active participation primarily refers to an inward participation of heart, mind, spirit, and voice in the context of the prayers, hymns, and offering of the Sacrifice of the Mass.

> To promote active participation, the people should be encouraged to take part by means of acclamations, responses, psalmody, antiphons, and songs, as well as by actions, gestures, and bodily attitudes. And at the proper times all should observe a reverent silence. (*CSL* 30)

> They should be instructed by God's word and be nourished at the table of the Lord's body; they should give thanks to God; by offering the Immaculate Victim, not only through the hands of the priest, but also with him, they should learn also to offer themselves; through Christ the Mediator, they should be drawn day by day into ever more perfect union with God and with each other. (*CSL* 48)

This line from paragraph 48—"by offering the Immaculate Victim, *not only through the hands of the priest, but also with him,* they should learn also to offer themselves"—is the true meaning and spirit of "active participation." The individual praying the Divine Mercy Chaplet engages the principle of active participation to mystically enter into the Sacrifice of the Mass, the sacrifice of the Lamb that was slain, as depicted in the book of Revelation (chapters 5–7). When we pray the Chaplet of Divine Mercy, we are participating mystically in the Eucharistic offering of the Mass—*Through him, and with him, and in him, O God, almighty Father, in the unity of the Holy Spirit, all glory and honor is yours, for ever and ever. Amen!*

The Chaplet offers us the opportunity of uniting ourselves to Jesus's perfect sacrifice "through the hands of the priest [and] with [the priest]." It is here that we can find ourselves standing before the Eternal Father, participating in the single greatest action that has ever taken place. Imagine yourself standing in the great throne room of heaven (Rv 4–5) and seeing the Lamb that was slain, and the heavenly court crying out, "To him who sits upon the throne and to the Lamb be blessing and honor and glory and might for ever and ever!" And the four living creatures said, "Amen!" and the elders fell down and worshiped" (Rv 5:13–14).

The Action of the Chaplet

Earlier I claimed that the Divine Mercy Chaplet is more powerful than the Rosary. Be not mistaken: the Rosary is an incredibly powerful prayer, and we should strive to pray it daily. But the difference between the Most Holy Rosary and the Chaplet of Divine Mercy is that the Rosary is primarily a *meditation*, while the Chaplet is an *action*. Just like the Chaplet, the Rosary is a powerful weapon that drives back Satan and converts souls. However, at the heart of the Rosary is the opportunity to meditate on the twenty mysteries of the life of Christ. Through Mother Mary's intercession ("pray for us sinners . . ."), these meditations nourish our minds and souls and lead us into deeper union with Jesus Christ. Deep meditation on the passion and death of Jesus is definitely possible, but only because you find yourself there. The Chaplet is, in its essence, an action; thus, when we pray it, we need to engage our imagination and see ourselves in that very action of offering Jesus to the Eternal Father.

Every mother has instructed her children to "pay attention to what you are doing." We should heed that advice when we pray the Chaplet. We should make sure we are not just routinely saying words, but that we are also, with great focus and intention, engaging in the *action of offering*.

Outside of Mass itself, because of this action that vivifies it, the Chaplet of Divine Mercy is the single most powerful prayer in our Catholic arsenal of prayers. Listen to Saint Faustina describe the power of the Divine Mercy prayers during a frightening vision she had of an angel she calls the "executor of divine wrath":

> In the evening, when I was in my cell, I saw an Angel, the executor of divine wrath. He was clothed in a dazzling robe, his face gloriously bright, a cloud beneath his feet. From the cloud, bolts of thunder and flashes of lightning were springing into his hands; and from his hand they were going forth, and only then were they striking the earth. . . . I began to implore the

Angel to hold off for a few moments, and the world would do penance. But my plea was a mere nothing in the face of the divine anger. Just then I saw the Most Holy Trinity. The greatness of Its majesty pierced me deeply, and I did not dare to repeat my entreaties. At that very moment I felt in my soul the power of Jesus' grace, which dwells in my soul. When I became conscious of this grace, I was instantly snatched up before the Throne of God. Oh, how great is our Lord and God and how incomprehensible His holiness! I will make no attempt to describe this greatness, because before long we shall all see Him as He is. I found myself pleading with God for the world with words heard interiorly.

The words with which I entreated God are these: Eternal Father, I offer You the Body and Blood, Soul and Divinity of Your dearly beloved son, Our Lord Jesus Christ for our sins and those of the whole world; for the sake of His sorrowful Passion, have mercy on us.

As I was praying in this manner, I saw the Angel's helplessness: he could not carry out the just punishment which was rightly due for sins. Never before had I prayed with such inner power as I did then. (*Diary* 474–75)

When you pray the Chaplet of Divine Mercy, you pray with the exact same power that Saint Faustina did. It is a sad excuse to say, "Her prayer was so powerful because she was chosen by God. She was a saint. I am not." Nonsense! She was so powerful because she offered what was the most powerful. She was powerful because she trusted in Jesus. She was powerful because she had faith. "I realize more and more how much every soul needs God's mercy throughout life and particularly at the hour of death. This chaplet (of Divine Mercy) mitigates God's anger, as He Himself told me" (*Diary* 1036).

It is incumbent for us to pick up the sword and shield of Divine Mercy and fight boldly for the kingdom of God. "If God is for us, who is against us?" (Rom 8:31). Can we give God a few minutes of our time each day to fight for the conversions of sinners? And not just one Chaplet each day but also being ready and willing to pray a single decade of the Chaplet, or at minimum, invoke the Mercy of God for particular needs or intentions throughout the day?

If we think of ourselves as soldiers for Christ and our days are spent patrolling in enemy territory, you would keep your weapon in your hand and be ready to fight at the first sign of danger. We should have our rosary beads in our hands at all times, ready for battle.

The Coming of the Last Days

One of the themes continually communicated throughout Saint Faustina's diary is that time is running out:

> **Write this: before I come as the Just Judge, I am coming first as the King of Mercy. Before the day of justice arrives, there will be given to people a sign in the heavens. . . . This will take place shortly before the last day.** (*Diary* 83)

You will prepare the world for My final coming.
(*Diary* 429)

(Words of the Blessed Virgin Mary to St. Faustina):
*"You have to speak to the world about His great mercy
and prepare the world for the Second Coming of Him
Who will come, not as a merciful Savior, but as a just
Judge. Oh, how terrible is that day! Determined is the
day of justice, the day of divine wrath. The angels tremble
before it. Speak to souls about this great mercy while it is
still the time for granting mercy."* (*Diary* 635)

**(My daughter) Speak to the world about My mercy;
let all mankind recognize My unfathomable mercy.
It is a sign for the end times; after it will come the
day of justice. While there is still time, let them have
recourse to the fount of My mercy; let them profit
from the Blood and Water which gushed forth for
them.** (*Diary* 848)

**Secretary of My mercy, write, tell souls about this
great mercy of Mine, because the awful day, the day
of My justice, is near."** (*Diary* 965)

These messages are not to create fear, but hope! We know
from Scripture that "where sin abounds grace abounds all
the more" (Rom 5:20). Therefore, in the end times, the most
difficult times, we can expect the greatest graces to be show-
ered down from heaven.

Our Lord chose Faustina as His instrument to convey
a message of great importance—namely, that the Divine
Mercy Chaplet has a very special role in these latter days,

primarily because of the power it enables one to pray with and the graces obtained for souls. The revelation of the Chaplet of Divine Mercy, a relatively new prayer in the life of the Church, is a great compliment to the Most Holy Rosary, which has been around for several centuries. Volumes of books have been written on the power of the Rosary, and countless saints have described it as one of their primary weapons in spiritual battles. So, too, I believe the Chaplet and the Rosary will be the two great weapons for our times, and ultimately the end times.

Our Lady of Akita's Warning

On October 13, 1973, the Blessed Virgin Mary appeared to Sister Agnes Sasagawa near Akita, Japan, conveying a series of messages. The following is what is referred to as the third secret of Akita, which was approved by the diocesan bishop.

> As I told you, if men do not repent and better themselves, the Father will inflict a terrible punishment on all humanity. It will be a punishment greater than the deluge, such as one will never have seen before. Fire will fall from the sky and will wipe out a great part of humanity, the good as well as the bad, sparing neither priests nor faithful. The survivors will find themselves so desolate that they will envy the dead. The only arms which will remain for you will be the Rosary and the Sign left by My Son. Each day recite the prayers of the Rosary. With the Rosary, pray for the Pope, the bishops and priests.

The work of the devil will infiltrate even into the
Church in such a way that one will see cardinals opposing cardinals, bishops against bishops. The priests who
venerate me will be scorned and opposed by their
confreres . . . churches and altars sacked; the Church
will be full of those who accept compromises and the
demon will press many priests and consecrated souls
to leave the service of the Lord.

The demon will be especially implacable against
souls consecrated to God. The thought of the loss of so
many souls is the cause of my sadness. If sins increase
in number and gravity, there will be no longer pardon
for them.

To put this quote in context, this message was given on
October 13, which is the anniversary of the Miracle of the
Sun, also known as the Miracle of Fatima. It was on October 13, 1917 that, in the presence of approximately seventy thousand people, over a ten-minute period, the sun
appeared to move in the sky and gave the impression it was
crashing to earth. The people who were there dove for cover
and cried out for mercy. This miracle was predicted by Our
Lady of Fatima, who had been appearing to three shepherd
children—Lucia Santos, and Francisco and Jacinta Marto—
in the remote hills of Portugal in the months leading up
to October 13. One of the primary messages of Our Lady's
visits was to pray the Rosary to save souls falling into hell.

Fifty-six years after Fatima, the Blessed Virgin Mary
appears in Japan on the anniversary of what appeared to be a
near occasion of fire falling from the sky and colliding with

the earth to give a warning about a chastisement that could come in the same form.

We can see that this message of Akita is truly prophetic and being fulfilled in our times. We are seeing in the various synods of the Church "cardinals opposing cardinals and bishops against bishop." In many churches, we see "compromise" as the norm, where the teachings of Jesus Christ are watered down, overlooked, or blatantly rejected. These very things are being fulfilled in our midst and we need to be attentive to the signs of the times. Specifically in relation to the last line of that revelation: "If sins increase in number and gravity, there will be no longer pardon for them." We must not let this time of mercy pass us by, when it will soon be too late to seek God's pardon for ourselves and our brothers and sisters.

How do we fight against this torrent that is being spewed out of the dragon's mouth? This third secret of Akita tells us. "The only arms [weapons] which will remain for you will be the Rosary and the Sign left by My Son. Each day recite the prayers of the Rosary." We see, yet again, the Rosary being referenced as a weapon. But what about "the Sign left by my son?" This reference can be interpreted in many ways. But speaking in terms of a Sign left by Jesus that would be a weapon, I would have to say it would be the sign of the cross; the sign of our redemption and defeat of death and all evil.

Spiritual directors and writers have all indicated that the cross, in its various forms, is a principal weapon against evil. Making the sign of the cross is a form of spiritual warfare, as is wearing one (a cross or crucifix). Of course, the source of this power comes not from our own hand making this sign, or the metal a crucifix is made from, but rather from the true cross erected on Calvary. The greatest spiritual combat that ever took place happened when Our Lord was crucified. Therefore, the Holy Mass, which makes present again the events of the Passion, extends those most powerful graces from Calvary into today. And if the Chaplet of Divine Mercy is an extension of the Mass, if it shares in that power, as we spoke about in the last chapter, then this prayer given to Faustina is likewise a powerful weapon to combat the devil.

This is why it is imperative to pray our Rosary and the Chaplet of Divine Mercy every day. It is not an option if we want our souls to be strong enough for the battle. Remember the power with which Saint Faustina prayed, rendering the executioner of divine wrath helpless? We too have that same power at our disposal!

Entering Deeper into Calvary

Section 476 of the Faustina's diary details the revelation of the Chaplet of Divine Mercy, both how to actually pray it and how it has the power to appease God's wrath.

> When I had said the prayer, in my soul I heard these words: **This prayer will serve to appease My wrath. You will recite . . . on the beads of the rosary . . . : First of all, you will say one OUR FATHER and HAIL MARY and the I BELIEVE IN GOD. Then on the OUR FATHER beads you will say the following words: "Eternal Father, I offer You the Body and Blood, Soul and divinity of Your dearly beloved**

Son, Our Lord Jesus Christ, in atonement for our sins and those of the whole world." On the HAIL MARY beads you will say the following words: "For the sake of His sorrowful Passion have mercy on us and on the whole world." In conclusion, three times you will recite these words: "Holy God, Holy Mighty One, Holy Immortal One, have mercy on us and on the whole world."

As you can see, the prayers of the Chaplet are easily said, memorized and quickly prayed in a few minutes. However, as we have been discussing, the Chaplet is not about just saying the words; *it is about entering into an event.* Earlier, we discussed the mystical reality of the Chaplet of Divine Mercy as an extension of the Liturgy of the Eucharist, which is an extension of the Mass, and how, when we pray the Chaplet of Divine Mercy, those same graces are made present. In this section, I would like to give you three images, or "modes of prayer," to help you enter more fully into the event and graces of Calvary. These modes of prayer will make you a powerful warrior with the Chaplet and assist your soul in preparation for the end times, whether that be Jesus's second coming or our own personal death and judgment (whichever comes first).

First Mode: Praying the Mass

There are a variety of meditations one can develop in relation to the Chaplet of Divine Mercy and the Mass. In this section, I will focus on two areas: the Great Doxology and the Lamb of God (*Agnus Dei*).

As we have been discussing, the primary prayer of the Chaplet of Divine Mercy is a direct extension of the Great Doxology of the Mass. This is the part of the Mass where the priest, holding the paten and chalice, elevates the Body and Blood of Jesus Christ and presents our Crucified Lord to the Eternal Father, proclaiming: "Through him, and with him, and in him, O God, almighty Father, in the unity of the Holy Spirit, all glory and honor is yours, for ever and ever." And the people proclaim, "Amen!"

If we look at this section of the Mass, the posture of the priest is important, the way his arms are extended, holding Jesus. This is the posture of *offering*. For our purposes, I want to take you back to the Old Testament, to the Battle of Refidim, where Moses and the Israelites fought the Amalekites:

> Then came Amalek and fought with Israel at Rephidim. And Moses said to Joshua, "Choose for us men, and go out, fight with Amalek; tomorrow I will stand on the top of the hill with the rod of God in my hand." So, Joshua did as Moses told him, and fought with Amalek; and Moses, Aaron, and Hur went up to the top of the hill. Whenever Moses held up his hand, Israel prevailed; and whenever he lowered his hand, Amalek prevailed. But Moses' hands grew weary; so, they took a stone and put it under him, and he sat upon it, and Aaron and Hur held up his hands, one on one side, and the other on the other side; so, his hands were steady until the going down of the sun. And Joshua mowed down Amalek and his people with the edge of the sword. (Ex 17:8–13)

There is much to be harvested from this passage. When you look at the timeline of this event, Moses and the Israelites had just left Egypt with nothing but the clothing on their backs, while Amalek and his army were well equipped for war. Moses essentially says to Joshua, "Pick some guys and go into battle and I will go the opposite direction, to the top of this really safe hill and pray for y'all." Not exactly what you want to hear from your friend. But, full of faith, Joshua leads the Israelites into battle, and he is a hero for doing so.

This battle against the Amalekites would have been lost if it were not for Joshua's heroics, but Aaron and Hur also deserve praise. These two faithful companions supported and held up the arms of Moses when he grew tired and weak. If Aaron and Hur did this for Moses, how much more can we do this for our Catholic priests, bishops, cardinals, and our Holy Father, the pope? It is easy for a priest to get weary, to slack off saying his prayers, to feel lonely, isolated, unsupported. Offering a decade of your daily Chaplet of Divine Mercy for the intentions of the ministers of the Church can renew them. Not just your local priest, but simultaneously, you can touch every priest in the world.

Yet it is not just about saying the decade worth of prayers for the priesthood; it is also about seeing yourself at Mass, participating in the great battle for souls. See the priest elevating our crucified Savior, holding the Chalice and Paten to God the Father. Imagine His weariness, His exhaustion of body and soul. Then (spiritually speaking) see yourself standing next to Him, holding on to and supporting one of His arms, and see the Blessed Virgin Mary holding up the other. Prayer transcends time and space, so in a single moment of prayer, you can be lifting up the entire priesthood, strengthening, healing, encouraging, enlightening, sanctifying them. There is no limit to what your prayers can do for the entire priesthood of the Church. Each person who prays in this way has the power and ability to fundamentally strengthen and sanctify the entire priesthood (and in just a minute or two).

This mode of prayer, supporting the arms of the priesthood, gives new life to the sentence in *Sacrosanctum Concilium*, "[the faithful] by offering the Immaculate Victim, not only through the hands of the priest, but also with him, they should learn also to offer themselves" (*CSL* 48). Could you imagine how connected and invested Aaron and Hur were on top of that mountain, not only to Moses but to Joshua, their relatives on the ground, and the entire nation of Israel? Israel could not have won without Moses, Aaron, and Hur, but Moses, Aaron, and Hur would have not made it through the day without the faithfulness of the Israelites walking into a battle where they were outnumbered and outgunned. So many times in our lives we feel the same way as the Israelites, but in the words of Saint Paul, "If God is for us, who can be against us?" (Rom 8:31).

Second Mode: At the Foot of the Cross

Another mode of praying the Chaplet of Divine Mercy is to enter into Jesus's crucifixion and death.

As I said earlier, the Rosary is a meditative prayer, while the Chaplet is an action, an offering. But as you can see, when we engage our imagination, *we can do both at the same time*. The key is to always keep the Eternal Father present in your mind's eye, to see yourself standing (or kneeling) before Him with Jesus in your arms in a gesture of offering, then build the scene around you.

The main scene we can build is Jesus's passion and death. It was on the cross that Jesus made His offering to God the Father, and there is much that transpired during the three-hour period. The more familiar you are with this moment in Jesus's life, the more you can get out of this mode of prayer. Other than reading the Gospel accounts, two simple ways of deepening your knowledge and experience of Calvary are to pray Saint Alphonsus Liguori's Stations of the Cross or meditate on the "seven last words of Jesus." Those last seven statements were:

- "Father, forgive them, for they know not what they do" (Lk 23:34).
- "Truly, I say to you, today you will be with me in paradise" (Lk 23:43).
- "Woman, behold your son. . . . Behold your mother" (Jn 19:26–27).
- "My God, my God, why have you forsaken me?" (Mt 27:46).
- "I thirst" (Jn 19:28).
- "It is finished" (Jn 19:30).
- "Father, into your hands I commend my spirit" (Lk 23:46).

When you meditate on Jesus's passion and death, you need not do anything other than stand there with Mary and the others and be attentive to Our Lord in His agony. Faustina's diary is filled with innumerable references of meditating on the passion of Jesus. In one section, Jesus says, **"There is more merit to one hour of meditation on My sorrowful Passion than there is to a whole year of flagellation that draws blood"** (*Diary* 369). Thus, as you stand there in the presence of Jesus's agony, you can imagine every wince of His body, every shockwave of pain as an offering for sin. Instead of seeing the horror and shame of the moment, see grace emanating and touching the souls that need it the most.

For anyone who has ever assisted a loved one in their last days, you will understand what this means. When we are at the bedside of someone who is dying, there is very little we can do other than small acts of love to keep them company and comfortable. Moistening their lips with ice wrapped in a towel, stroking their hair, holding their hand; anything that lets them know you are there and they are not alone comforts them in this process. It is the same with Jesus in His agony. If we stand at the foot of the cross with indifference, we gain nothing. But if we stand there with great love and attention, it changes everything. Especially when we bring Him people or events that need His Mercy.

This is reflected in the structuring of the Divine Mercy Novena that is normally prayed Good Friday through Divine Mercy Sunday. This novena was given to us directly by Our Lord Himself and, per His request, has us bringing Jesus different groups of people each day.

Jesus tells us: "Today bring to me . . ."

Day 1	all mankind, especially sinners.
Day 2	the souls of priests and religious.
Day 3	all devout and faithful souls.
Day 4	the pagans and those who do not yet know [Jesus].
Day 5	the souls of those who have separated themselves from My Church.
Day 6	the meek and humble souls and the souls of little children.
Day 7	the souls who especially venerate and glorify Jesus's mercy.
Day 8	the souls who are in the prison of purgatory
Day 9	the souls who have become lukewarm.

Continuing with our meditation on the Passion, we can reflect on the piercing of Jesus's side and the taking down from the cross. "When Jesus had received the vinegar, he said, 'It is finished'; and he bowed his head and gave up his spirit. . . . In order to prevent the bodies from remaining on the cross on the sabbath . . . one of the soldiers pierced his side with a spear, and at once there came out blood and water" (Jn 19:30–34).

The flowing of Christ's blood and water from His pierced side is the central theme of the Divine Mercy image. In addition, it has sacramental meaning: the water is a clear symbol for baptism, and the blood for the Eucharist. The Church Fathers tell us that the Church was "born" at the piercing of Jesus's side; this was the moment where the sacraments received their power.

One of the most powerful ways of praying while reflecting on the precious blood and water is to imagine all those who have left the Catholic faith—your family, friends, even strangers—all those who no longer receive the sacraments. See yourself bringing these people to the cross as the centurion pierces Jesus's side. And just as in that moment when the sacraments of the Church received their power, see the souls of these people jolted back to life. For these people, think of this mode of prayer as a "divine defibrillator"; we awaken in dead souls the power of God through His sacraments. When we mystically lead people to the cross like this, we pray one day they will make the same proclamation as the centurion: "This Man truly was the Son of God!" (Mt 27:54, Mk 15:39).

Another way of "praying Calvary" is by seeing Jesus now taken down from the cross and placed in the hands of His Mother. Imagine the weight of this moment, as the lifeless body of her Son lies in her arms. Imagine yourself there as the Blessed Virgin Mary looks directly at you and invites you to come to her and Jesus. As you come close, our Mother stands and begins to place Jesus in your arms too. She supports His weight as you place your arms around Him. As the two of you hold Him, the skies open and the Eternal Father reveals Himself. And together, you and the Blessed Mother elevate the body of her Son and offer Him to the Eternal Father.

Third Mode: The Lamb That Was Slain

Imagine yourself standing among the saints and angels in heaven looking down upon the calamity that exists in the world as a result of sin and the work of the devil. Imagine the just "wrath of the Eternal Father that is rightly due for sin" (*Diary* 474), and see yourself arise from the mists of the heavenly hosts and approach the throne where the Lamb resides, as though slain (see Rv 5:6). See yourself pick up the Lamb and approach the Eternal Father and offer Him this perfect sacrifice of innocence, obedience, and love. And just as Saint Faustina rendered the executioner of divine wrath helpless, so too does our Heavenly Father's countenance change from wrath to satisfaction. Your offering has granted the world the necessary graces for conversion.

Fulfilling Our Obligation

These modes of prayer are simply techniques of entering into the event of Calvary more fully, which will allow us to be as effective as Saint Faustina in our prayers. We must take Our Lord's words seriously, that we will do greater miracles than He (Jn 14:12). With our prayer, fasting, penance, and almsgiving, we have the spiritual weapons necessary to lead many souls back to Christ. We not only have the opportunity to do this, *we have the obligation*. Once Saint Faustina asked how He could tolerate so many sins and crimes and not punish those who committed them. The Lord answered, "I have eternity for punishing [these], and so I am prolonging the time of mercy for the sake of [sinners]. But woe to them if they do not recognize this time of My visitation.

My daughter, secretary of My mercy, your duty is not only to write about and proclaim My mercy, but also to beg for this grace for them, so that they too may glorify My mercy" (*Diary* 1160).

Responding to Jesus's request to "fight like a knight" (*Diary* 1760) is more important now than ever before. Time is running out. We should live like the first century Christians who expected Jesus's second coming was imminent. It was September 13, 1935 that the Chaplet was given to Faustina; we are quickly approaching the one hundredth anniversary of that date. It is clear that we are living in a world that is spinning out of control. I am not prophesying that something will happen, but there are too many other sinful and biblically prophetic things happening in our world not take these prophetic revelations seriously. Thus, let us respond to Jesus's warnings not only by praying the Chaplet of Divine Mercy ourselves, and by encouraging others to pray it.

The Chaplet and Protestants

In my reversion from Agnosticism back to Catholicism, I spent some time attending Protestant and non-denominational churches. One of the most notable questions I remember being asked was, "Have you been washed in the Blood of the Lamb?" As I have immersed myself in the Divine Mercy message, I cannot help but reflect on the parallels between this question and the rays that emit from the Divine Mercy image, and mystically from the Divine Mercy Chaplet.

Many Protestants look down on formal prayer as the mindless repetition of words. They cite Scripture to prove this: "And in praying do not heap up empty phrases as the Gentiles do; for they think that they will be heard for their many words" (Mt 6:7). However, I have found that if I have a relationship with a non-Catholic Christian and I offer them the Surrender Novena or the Litany of Humility, or some other formal prayer, they receive it with great appreciation. They will actually say the prayers and find tremendous value in the sacred words. In my experience, I have found most Christians are just looking for what works to create a deeper relationship with Jesus Christ and to fight for the needs and souls of their family members, friends, and of the whole world. Many will receive a Catholic resource with reservation, but if they find that it works for them, they keep it in their war-chest.

I think the best example of this is Pastor Rick Warren of Saddleback Church in California. In 2014, Warren was interviewed on EWTN's "The World Over" with Raymond Arroyo. During that conversation, Warren indicated that he watched EWTN more than any other Christian network and that his favorite show was the Divine Mercy Chaplet. Here is the exact quote from that interview: "One of my favorite shows [on EWTN] is the Chaplet of Divine Mercy. Which, I love. And when I have a very stressful day, I'll come home, I've got it taped, and Kay [wife] and I will put it on and sit back, relax and worship; and in that time of reflection, meditation, quietness, I find myself renewed and restored."[20]

---

[20] EWTN. YouTube, EWTN, 10 Apr. 2014, https://www.youtube.com/watch?v=dVCY8pW-ACs.

I believe this kind of testimony creates an opportunity for evangelizing through the Chaplet. Very simply, if your non-Catholic friend or relation has shared that they are stressed or overburdened or having a difficult day, you can ask them if they would like to pray together. You do not have to pray the entire Chaplet; you can just pray a single decade and invite them to give the response:

Leader's Part	Responder's Part
(One time): Eternal Father, I offer you the Body, Blood, Soul and Divinity of your dearly beloved Son, Our Lord Jesus Christ,	in atonement for our sins and those of the whole world.
(Ten times): For the sake of His sorrowful Passion,	have mercy on us and on the whole world.

Do not feel obligated to give a detailed explanation of the Chaplet or its history. Just pray with them and keep it simple. You can show them a picture of the Divine Mercy Image, telling them that the repetitive recitation of this prayer invites what we pray into our lives. In this case, we are standing together at Calvary during Jesus's crucifixion, and as we can see in the image, it is the Blood and Water that is gushing forth. So, for the length of these prayers, we are placing ourselves at the foot of the cross and being washed in the Blood of the Lamb.

The Chaplet is a great resource for evangelization because we just get to let God be God in these moments. If a non-Catholic invites Jesus Christ into his life and allows himself to be washed in the Blood of the Lamb, as given us in the Divine Mercy Chaplet, I can only imagine (based on the promises in the diary) that God will either begin, or continue, to work powerfully in his life.

Never be afraid to share your faith by praying with another person or giving out a Divine Mercy prayer card. You have no idea how God will use that small act.

The Word of Christ on the Chaplet

This was a rather long chapter, but I hope you see now the power behind this prayer. To further stress this power, let us close by reading and meditating on some of Christ's words to Faustina about the Chaplet of Divine Mercy.

> **Whoever will recite it will receive great mercy at the hour of death. Priests will recommend it to sinners as their last hope of salvation. Even if there were a sinner most hardened, if he were to recite this chaplet only once, he would receive grace from My infinite mercy.** (*Diary* 687)

> **By** [the Divine Mercy] **novena, I will grant every possible grace to souls.** (*Diary* 796)

> **My daughter, encourage souls to say the chaplet which I have given to you. It pleases Me to grant everything they ask of Me by saying the chaplet. When hardened sinners say it, I will fill their souls with peace, and the hour of their death will be a happy one. . . . Write that when they say this chaplet in the presence of the dying, I will stand between**

My Father and the dying person, not as the just Judge but as the merciful Savior. (*Diary* 1541)

Say the chaplet I have taught you, and the storm will cease. . . . And I heard the words: **Through the chaplet you will obtain everything, if what you ask for is compatible with My will.** (*Diary* 1731)

PART III

OTHER AIDS FOR BATTLE

CHAPTER 7

THE MOST HOLY ROSARY

The Rosary as a Spiritual Weapon

There are countless books in the Catholic treasury that chronicle the power of the Most Holy Rosary. Two that are at the top of my own personal list are *The Secret of the Rosary*, by Saint Louis De Montfort, and *Champions of the Rosary*, by Donald Calloway. Saint Louis De Montfort's book is said to be the best book ever written about the Rosary, while Father Calloway has compiled a treasure that frames a thorough history of the Rosary in the first part, then, in part two, he shares the stories of twenty-six holy men and women and their thoughts, teachings, and experiences with the Rosary.

Both books are powerhouses, not just by informing us, but by edifying us and increasing our faith in the power of the Rosary. The cover of *Champions of the Rosary* includes a shield and swords, emphasizing the Rosary's role in the midst of this spiritual war. This shows us how the Rosary can be a powerful spiritual weapon.

In this chapter, I want to open up for us just a few basic principles to encourage us to seek Mother Mary's protection through the Rosary in the battle for our souls.

105

Mary as Mama Bear

In my first book, *Why Be Catholic?*, I dedicated a good portion of text to the maternity of the Blessed Virgin Mary and her role as the mother of all humanity. Instead of going through that again, I will give you the simplest way of understanding how Mary is our mother.

First, Jesus came to establish a covenant; a covenant creates a family-like bond. The covenant was ratified with the sacrifice of Jesus. Two things happened at Jesus's death: our redemption and divine adoption. So, through the sacrifice of Jesus, we become sons and daughters of God the Father, and Jesus becomes our brother. And if God is our Father and Jesus is our brother, who is our mother? The Blessed Virgin Mary of course!

Even if a skeptic were to acknowledge her maternal role in the Christian family, he still might ask why we pray to her. The most direct answer points us to the fourth commandment: "Honor your father and mother." One way we honor our spiritual mother is to talk and spend time with her. In addition, going to Mother Mary conforms to the teaching of Jesus, who said, "Truly, I say to you, unless you turn and become like children, you will never enter the kingdom of heaven" (Mt 18:3). A child is totally dependent on the family for everything. He loves his mother, and she loves him.

In our context of spiritual warfare, I want to make it very practical for us. I started this book with the Scripture passage: "Then the dragon was angry with the woman, and went off to make war on the rest of her offspring, on those who keep the commandments of God and bear testimony to

Jesus" (Rv 12:17). The woman in this passage who is at war with the dragon is Mary. Mary is fighting for her children. When she sees the dragon making war on her children, she becomes like a fierce mama bear defending her cubs.

Over the centuries, there have been countless witnesses of a meek and tender mother turning into an aggressive warrior to protect their child, women who would not hesitate to put themselves in harm's way or even sacrifice their own lives for their children. This behavior is not learned; God built this behavior into the human condition. Thus, if this is the way a natural mother loves and protects her own children, how much more does our supernatural mother love and protect her children?

We must recognize that one of the best tactics in spiritual warfare is running to Mother Mary for protection. How do we do this practically? By picking up our rosaries.

The Prayers of the Rosary

Many Protestants claim that by praying the Rosary, we are worshipping Mary. There are entire volumes written refuting this claim, and at the heart of the dialogue is the distinction between *veneration* and *adoration*. Where adoration relates to the total and consuming reverence due to God, veneration applies to the honor and respect due to humans.

The prayers of the Rosary are the words (or matter), but the form (or substance) of the Rosary is the meditation on the twenty biblical mysteries of the life of Christ. Many have referred to the Rosary as the "pocket gospel" because it is a prayer that serves as a series of biblical meditations. As we pray, we meditate on the most profound moments from the lives of Jesus and Mary (the Annunciation, the Nativity, the Crucifixion, the Resurrection, etc.). If our Protestant brothers and sisters understood the scriptural roots of the Rosary, they would be more willing to accept it, perhaps even pray it.

The Creed

When we dissect the prayers of the Rosary, we find even greater power. The Apostles' Creed, which is widely under-estimated in its power, professes the twelve principal articles of our Catholic faith. The creed can make all of hell tremble if said devoutly and intentionally. Just think about what the words "I believe" mean, and all that we are saying we believe in. When we pray the creed, we are pronouncing our belief in God's Divine Revelation and plan for all of humanity. It is an affirmation of the teachings of Jesus Christ and a total rejection of Satan and his lies. This prayer alone is a war-hammer.

The Our Father

The Our Father is another prayer of the Rosary. Again, vol-umes have been written about the seven perfect petitions included in this prayer, but it is sufficient to say that because these are the very words of Jesus Himself, there is tremen-dous power in them. In addition, with every Our Father offered, we are praying to forgive and be forgiven, to be protected from temptation and to be delivered from evil. Remember the old saying, "An ounce of prevention is bet-ter than a pound of cure?" Well, praying the Our Father, praying for protection from temptation, is highly recommended to avoid the snares of the devil, to avoid even falling into sin. Don't say these words idly or without thought— truly believe in them!

The Hail Mary

Next, we have the Hail Mary. The first half of the prayer is scriptural, the words coming from both the angel Gabriel at the Annunciation, and Elizabeth at the Visitation:

> "Hail Mary, full of grace, the Lord is with thee . . ." (Lk 1:28)

> "Blessed art thou among women, and blessed is the fruit of thy womb . . ." (Lk 1:42)

Though it was the archangel Gabriel who was the first to proclaim Mary as "full of grace," we read that he was "sent from God" to make this proclamation (Lk 1:26). Thus, there are a few things at work here. First, these are not Gabriel's words, but the very words of God Himself! Second, "Hail" is a royal greeting, prefiguring Mary's queenship of heaven after her assumption. So, just by praying this first part of the Hail Mary, we are invoking the very words of God and affirming the queenship of the Blessed Virgin Mary.

Following this, Mary gave her *fiat*, her yes to God: "Let it be done to me according to your Word" (Lk 1:38). She then conceived by the Holy Spirit and the Word was made flesh. When we pray the Hail Mary, we hope that the Word of God is conceived in us spiritually and that we come to know the Word made man.

The next part of the Hail Mary was also spoken by God through one of His instruments. Though it was Elizabeth, at the Visitation, who spoke the words, we read that she was "filled with the Holy Spirit" when she exclaimed with a loud cry, "Blessed are you among women, and blessed is the fruit of your womb" (Lk 1:42). Again, recognizing that this part of the Hail Mary is not only directly from Sacred Scripture but is composed of the words of God Himself should fill us with great awe and reverence when we pray them. The third person of the Most Holy Trinity came upon Mary's cousin, filling her with the inspiration to speak these words that have been repeated countless times for the last two millennia.

The power and significance of these moments are lost on many, including zealous Christian believers. But thanks be to God they have been memorialized by Catholics in the Hail Mary prayer. Satan hates the Blessed Virgin Mary more than any other creature because he never had any claim on her; on account of her sinlessness, he could not touch her in any way. This makes the words of the Hail Mary like stakes in the heart of Satan.

Of course, the word that drives the biggest stake into his heart is the Holy Name of Jesus, which serves as the apex of the Hail Mary. "Blessed is the fruit of thy womb, *Jesus.*" The name of Jesus is powerful in itself. "Therefore, God has highly exalted him and bestowed on him the name which is above every name, that at the name of Jesus every knee should bow, in heaven and on earth and under the earth, and every tongue confess, to the glory of God the Father, that Jesus Christ is Lord" (Phil 2:10–11).

As one blogger writes:[21]

> We are to worship in the Name of Jesus.
>
> We are to pray in the Name of Jesus.
>
> We are to welcome people in the Name of Jesus.
>
> We can command demons in the Name of Jesus.
>
> The Name of Jesus is powerful in healing.
>
> We are to preach in Name of Jesus.
>
> We can suffer for the Name of Jesus

After we proclaim the Holy Name, the second half of the Hail Mary begins with an important acknowledgment. "Holy Mary, Mother of God . . ." With these words, we proclaim that Jesus Christ is God and Lord, and that God chose to come into the world through a woman, through this specific woman. Clearly, if God held Mary in high regard, shouldn't we? And finally, the prayer concludes with a petition, a request, that our Mother and Queen intercede for us: "Pray for us sinners, now and at the hour of our death." With these words, we recognize the hold that sin has on us, and by this statement, we are indirectly pronouncing our need for a Savior. And when do we need this intercession? When do we need this Savior? At the two most important moments of our lives: now and at the hour of our death. The

---

[21] "Weapons of Spiritual Warfare - The Name of Jesus," God's Word Is Flawless, accessed 26 Dec. 2021, http://godswordisflawless.org /Weapons%20of%20Spiritual%20Warfare,%20The%20Name%20 of%20Jesus.html.

word "now" invites the queenship of Mary and the reign of Jesus Christ into whatever moment you find yourself.

Recently, I was at the airport with one of my best friends to pick up his daughter from an international trip. As my friend was pulling the luggage off the baggage turn, he collapsed and turned as gray as the concrete floor. The situation was very touch and go as we cried for help and worked to stabilize him. In those moments, I was able to anoint and absolve him and offer him apostolic pardon before the ambulance arrived to rush him to the hospital. His daughters and I followed in the family car, and as we drove, we prayed decades of the Rosary. You can imagine how emotionally charged that drive was; we didn't even attempt to announce a mystery or to meditate as we prayed. But you can bet that each time we said the word *"now,"* it was said with urgency and fervor! This situation mercifully had a happy ending; by God's grace and Mother Mary's intercession, their dad pulled through and made a full recovery.

Praying for us "at the hour of our death" is also a tremendous request and weapon in the greatest moment of spiritual warfare. It was once common knowledge that the last moments of life were the greatest time of spiritual trial and attack (now it is too often assumed that everyone who dies is on an easy path to heaven). When a person is the weakest and most vulnerable, Satan's attacks are the fiercest. He knows the state of the soul about to cross over, and if the soul is not in a state of grace, it is his. Diabolic legions prowl about doing everything possible to prevent God's mercy from saving the soul. If the person is in a state of grace, the devil will harass the individual all the more, trying to sow seeds of discord, doubt, confusion, trying to thieve the person's faith in the last moments of life. This concept may be foreign to those of us who are strong in our faith, but there are a great number of Christian faithful who are barely hanging on. A solid assault of the devil could be their downfall. Thus, this prayer to our spiritual Mother asking for her intercession, asking for her to be at our side at the most critical moment of our lives, is a powerful defense.

The Fatima Prayer

Lastly, there is a prayer that follows each decade of the Rosary. It is known as "the Fatima Prayer" because it was given to the three shepherd children by Our Lady of Fatima in 1917. "O my Jesus, forgive us our sins, save us from the fires of hell; lead all souls to heaven, especially those in most need of Thy mercy." This powerful prayer invokes Jesus Christ Himself to help us turn from our sins, turn from our evil ways, asking for the grace to be put on the sure path to heaven, for both us and those in the greatest need. These petitions are like a volley of arrows that sink deep into Satan and the diabolic legions. They are a refutation of hell, a request that hell be left empty and heaven be filled with all our souls. We must not underestimate the power of this prayer considering it came to us through the lips of the Blessed Virgin Mary.

The Rosary's Power in Battle

The Most Holy Rosary has played a role in many battles over the last five hundred years, specifically battles when Christendom was under attack by Muslims, Communists, or other hostile empires. Whether it is the Church militant praying the Rosary at the behest of the Holy Father or actual soldiers calling out to the Blessed Virgin Mary with their rosary beads, below serves as a partial list of battles and conflicts where the praying of the Rosary helped defeat the powers of evil (brief information is provided here, but you are encouraged to read more about these on your own):

- The Battle of Lapanto (1571): The great naval battle where the outnumbered and outgunned Holy League defeated the Ottoman Empire. There are stories of Pope Pius having meetings in the Vatican while the Holy League battled, and at one point, he received a vision and stopped what he was doing to announce that the Holy League had won a great victory. The official announcement of the battle results did not arrive in Rome until many days later.

- The Battle of Vienna (1683): As 300,000 Turks were advancing on the Venetian capital, Pope Innocent ordered that Rosaries be recited in the religious houses and churches of Rome. Poland's king, John Sobieski, started his army's march into battle on the feast of the Assumption, August 15, 1683. The small army hit the Turks so hard in a surprise attack, it forced them to flee.

- The Battle of Belgrade (1717): Austrian troops captured the important city of Belgrade from the Ottoman Empire. The Church invoked a Rosary crusade and Prince Eugene of Savoy led his army of 91,000 soldiers against 160,000 Turks. After the miraculous victory, Pope Clement XI changed the feast of Our Lady of Victory to the feast of "Our Lady of the Holy Rosary" to be celebrated by the universal Church.

- Russian occupation of Austria (1955): After a Rosary crusade by the Catholics of Austria, the Russians leave only a month later.

- Brazil comes under communist control (1964): Fr. Patrick Payton invokes a Rosary crusade in which 5.5 million participated; the communist government falls within a year.

- Communist government takes over Portugal (1974): Again, a communist government takes over a country; in response, four teachers called for a Rosary crusade, and in less than twelve months, the government falls.

- The Islamist terrorist organization Boko Haram attempts to carry out genocide in Nigeria (2016): Bishop Oliver Doeme receives a vision of Jesus handing him a sword, saying, "Boko Haram is gone" three times. The sword then turns into a rosary. A Rosary crusade is launched, and in less than two years, Boko Haram is gone.

This is only a small list of such stories. Plenty more throughout history exist. These stories put the power of the Rosary on display in earthly battles; how much more, then, will it aid us in our spiritual struggles!

Pope Pius XII referred to the Rosary as the "slingshot of David." The Most Holy Rosary is as much a weapon as it is a shield. But let us not forget that it is also a lasso that we can use to pull down evil or rescue hostages of the devil. In the face of the greatest evils the world has ever seen, the Rosary has been present and brought forth victory. The most effective weapon is the one you use; if you fight with the weapons God has given, you will be victorious. Make a pledge now:

Commit to praying the Most Holy Rosary every day.

Commit to praying the Chaplet of Divine Mercy every day.

CHAPTER 8

Praying a Spiritual Mass

The Devotional Prayer of a "Spiritual Mass"

Participating in the Holy Sacrifice of the Mass is to be present at Calvary as the consummation of Jesus's perfect sacrifice overcomes sin and death. Participating at Mass is participating in the greatest battle of all time, where Jesus on the cross is not the victim but the hunter, a warrior. "The Ambush Predator has drawn the prey. He will enter into death and, from the inside, destroy its power. Jesus on the cross is not the poor, helpless victim, and he is not the hunted. Jesus on the cross is the aggressor and the hunter."[22]

Keeping the Mass alive in our mind, heart, and devotional life can help us better enter into the actual Holy Sacrifice of the Mass on the days we are able to attend, and make us more effective warriors for Jesus Christ in our daily lives.

What I am about to present to you in this chapter is a subject I first preached on Divine Mercy Sunday in 2013. The concept of making a spiritual Mass is similar to making a spiritual communion, what we do when we cannot physically be present at Mass. This has more significance now than ever before, since, as we saw during the COVID-19

---

[22] Fr. John Riccardo and Scott Hahn, *Rescued: The Unexpected and Extraordinary News of the Gospel* (Word Among Us Press, 2020), 114.

pandemic, the joy of attending and celebrating Mass could be taken away from us in a blink. There were times in the past when I would say, "The day may come when the Mass is not available or is taken away from us." Never in my lifetime did I actually think that would happen. As much as we hope it doesn't happen again, it very well could.

It should be noted that all that follows is strictly for devotional purposes only and is *not* a substitute for attending holy Mass, especially on Sundays or on holy days of obligation.

How to Make a Spiritual Mass

The Mass is comprised of two parts: the Liturgy of the Word and the Liturgy of the Eucharist. In previous chapters, we have shown how the Chaplet is an extension of Liturgy of the Eucharist. For this concept of making or "praying" a spiritual Mass, we will view the Rosary as a parallel to the Liturgy of the Word. Just as we are nourished by the Sacred Scriptures in the Liturgy of the Word at Mass, we are also nourished by the meditation on the Gospels while praying the Rosary. Thus, very simply, the practice of praying a spiritual Mass would be to treat the Rosary as the Liturgy of the Word, then go directly into the Divine Mercy Chaplet as the Liturgy of the Eucharist.

The practice, of course, requires rosary beads, but also access to the Mass readings of the day (which can always be found on the USCCB website), and about thirty minutes of time to pray. For this spiritual Liturgy of the Word, one can pray the prayers of the Rosary while meditating on the daily Mass readings. To prepare, simply review the Mass readings of the day and identify how you would like to divide them into five segments, one segment for each decade. As you pray each decade of the Rosary, meditate on the readings for the day (as opposed to the normal mysteries of the Rosary). When you reach the end of the fifth decade, pray the Hail, Holy Queen and "O God, whose only begotten Son" prayer, just as you would under normal circumstances. At this point in the Rosary, we normally conclude with praying for the needs and intentions of our Holy Father by saying an additional Our Father, Hail Mary, and Glory Be, followed by the sign of the cross. Instead of those three prayers, however, you can transition directly into the Chaplet by saying the Our Father, Hail Mary, and Apostles Creed (which are the opening prayers of the Chaplet), then go into the Chaplet's proper prayers. Thus, we have moved from the Liturgy of the Word to the Liturgy of the Eucharist.

To help you see it more succinctly, here are the prayers of a spiritual Mass in list form:

- Sign of the Cross
- Apostles' Creed
- Our Father
- Three Hail Marys
- Five decades meditating on the daily readings
- Hail, Holy Queen and "O God, whose ..."

(Treat the next three prayers as a bridge from the Rosary to the Chaplet, similar to Mass, where, after the homily, the Creed and prayers of the faithful are said.)

- Our Father, Hail Mary, and Apostles' Creed
- Five Decades of the Chaplet

- Prior to concluding the Chaplet with the *"Holy God, Holy Mighty One, Holy Immortal One,"* take a few moments to make an act of Spiritual Communion with the Blessed Sacrament. One can do this by praying: *"My Jesus, I believe that You are present in the Most Blessed Sacrament. I love You above all things, and I desire to receive You into my soul. Since I cannot now receive you sacramentally, come at least spiritually into my heart. I embrace You as if You were already there, and I unite myself wholly to You. Never permit me to be separated from You."* [23]

- When you are finished, spend some time in silence, as if you had actually received Jesus in Holy Communion. Let your heart speak to His. Profess your love and gratitude to Him, then ask of Him what you wish.

- After a period of thanksgiving for the spiritual graces received, conclude the spiritual Mass by reciting the closing prayers of the Chaplet. Say three times: *"Holy God, Holy Mighty One, Holy Immortal One, Have Mercy on us and on the whole World."*

For those who are new to the term "spiritual communion," it is a formal prayer, or prayer of the heart, that we make when we are unable to physically receive Jesus in Holy Communion. Saint Thomas Aquinas says, "[It] is an ardent desire to receive Jesus in the Most Blessed Sacrament at Mass and in lovingly embracing Him as if we had actually received Him." Though we are bound by the sacraments, *God is not.*

---

[23] Prayer from Saint Alphonus Liguori.

Thus, in the event of having the authentic desire for Jesus, but being unable to receive Him, a spiritual communion is the next best thing for receiving Our Lord and the graces associated with Holy Communion. In a spiritual communion, we come back to Him by turning our heart to His, and saying, "Lord, I wish to experience You in my heart. I invite You in. I wish You to be Lord of my life, love of my heart." The opportunity we have before us is to enter into a deep spiritual communion with Our Lord, uniting ourselves with Him, through Word and Sacrifice, in this devotional act of a spiritual Mass.

As previously stated, going to Mass is not about receiving Jesus; it is about the worship of God the Father, through the sacrifice of Jesus, in the Holy Spirit. Praying a spiritual Mass is a means of prayer that reflects the format of the actual Mass and shows great commitment on the part of the individual to give God his very best, in the event one cannot participate in an actual Mass. This devotional act takes preparation, time, focus, and emotional and spiritual energy; it very much reflects our participation in an ordinary Mass. You can be certain that it is meritorious in the eyes of our Eternal Father, who blesses and rewards those who love Him.

CHAPTER 9

HOW TO PRAY THE MASS— THE DIVINE MERCY ELEMENTS

Participating in the Great Victory

The greatest and most epic battle of human history took place on Calvary, where Jesus Christ conquered sin and death. Satan and his diabolic legions are defeated; therefore, it stands to reason that the most effective spiritual warfare is when we attend and participate in Holy Mass. We engage in this spiritual warfare when we bring our own "world" with us to Mass: our family, friends, all those we know, our work, problems, joys, intercessions, and intentions. We literally bring everything we are and experience to Calvary, where Jesus is victorious over all works of the devil, sin, and evil.

However, our ability to receive the greatest graces is directly related to our personal presence and participation in the Sacred Mysteries. In this chapter, I would like to open up for you some of the mystical and practical dimensions of the Mass. In my first book, "Why Be Catholic?", I dedicated an entire chapter to walking the reader through the Mass. In this book, I want to focus on the two parts of the Mass that directly relate to the Divine Mercy Chaplet and the Divine Mercy Image: the Great Doxology and the fraction of the sacred Host after the *Agnus Dei* (Lamb of God). Prior to

addressing these two parts of the Mass, I would like to outline how to pray them (and their Divine Mercy relation) by
helping frame how we should approach the Mass itself.

Our Approach to Mass

One of the observations I have made in this book is that the
Divine Mercy Chaplet is a mystical extension of the Liturgy
of the Eucharist of the Mass. Through "active participation,"
the lay faithful unite themselves through the hands of the
priest in the re-presented sacrificial offering of Christ crucified to the Father. From this, mankind receives the free gift of
redemption and divine adoption. So yes, both the Mass and
the Chaplet are direct conversations with God the Father.
In all reality, the Mass has an audience of *one*—that is, God
the Father; and by extension, the Divine Mercy Chaplet also
has an audience of one. At Mass, the congregation is not
the "audience"; rather, the congregation would be the "per-
formers," or, more appropriately, the worshipers. The laity do
not come to Mass to receive; they are obligated to come to
Mass every Sunday and holy day to *give*: to give their perfect
adoration and worship to the Father. So, before we get into
Great Doxology and fraction of the sacred Host, I would like
to dedicate a few words to the proper approach to the Mass.

In my travels as a missionary preacher, I have heard it said
on multiple occasions by a devout and loving Catholic, "I
cannot wait to go to Mass and receive Jesus." I love this. I
have no problem whatsoever with an individual who hun-
gers to receive Jesus and to be loved by Him and love Him
back! Jesus desires this in the greatest way. However, Holy

Mass is not about receiving communion. If you study the Mass, you will notice that the vast majority of the prayers of the Mass are directed to God the Father. Only a few times do we directly address Jesus in the Mass, and those parts are found in the second half of the *Gloria* and after the consecration of the sacred species:

In the *Kyrie*:

- Lord have Mercy, Christ have Mercy, Lord have Mercy.

In the *Gloria*:

- At the midpoint, the *Gloria* transitions focus from the Father to the Son:

  Lord God, heavenly King,
  O God, almighty Father.
  Lord Jesus Christ, Only Begotten Son,
  Lord God, Lamb of God, Son of the Father . . .

After the Consecration:

- The Mystery of Faith (we speak to Jesus on the altar).
- "For the kingdom and the power and glory are yours now and forever."
- Lord Jesus Christ, who said to your Apostles: Peace I leave you, my peace I give you, look not on our sins, but on the faith of your Church, and graciously grant her peace and unity in accordance with your will. Who live and reign for ever and ever.
- Lamb of God, you take away the sins of the world, have mercy on us . . . have mercy on us . . . grant us peace.

- Lord, I am not worthy that you should enter under my roof, but only say the word and my soul shall be healed.

Holy Mass is not about receiving communion, it is about worshiping God the Father through, with, and in the sacrifice of His Son, in the Holy Spirit. So, every Catholic and every Christian should have the mentality, "I cannot wait to go to Mass to worship the Father!"

When the laity come to Mass, they effectively have a "job" to do. Their job is to participate with full heart and full voice at each part of the liturgy. If the congregation has a response to say, you should say it with intentionality and fullness of heart. One of the worst parts of being a priest is hearing half-hearted responses at each part of the Mass. I do not say it is the worst because of the way it makes me feel, but because disinterested responses displease the Father. Imagine your father very intentionally saying, "I love you," and you respond without eye contact and with a very weak or disinterested "I love you too." How would that make him feel? Mass is so much more than just a series of responses; it is about allowing heart to speak to Heart. It should be filled with passion and emotion. So every time we prepare for Mass and enter a church, we should have the mentality of a performer who has a job to do and strive to do our part with excellence. Because when we give our very best to God, God will not be outdone in generosity. We see this generosity in action in the Mass itself. After we have united ourselves, through the hands of the priest, in the offering of the Body, Blood, Soul, and Divinity of Jesus Christ to the

Father (the Great Doxology), the Father then feeds us with His Son in Holy Communion.

The Great Doxology is the height of the Mass; it is the reason we have come. In this moment, the priest has said the consecration, concluded the Eucharistic Prayers. He then lifts the up the Body, Blood, Soul, and Divinity of Jesus Christ and makes the great offering proclamation to God the Father: "Through him, and with him, and in him, O God, almighty Father, in the unity of the Holy Spirit, all glory and honor is yours, for ever and ever." And, with all of their inner strength and heartfelt love, the people proclaim, "Amen." The people uniting themselves with the offering of the priest is the "active participation." At each Great Doxology, you can imagine the arms of the priest lifting the prayers and intentions of those present, united to the sacrifice. You can also imagine that every Divine Mercy Chaplet around the world that is being prayed is being united to this moment. Just as Aaron and Hur lifted up the arms of Moses, so you also assist not only the priest at Mass but every single person in the world praying and uniting themselves to Jesus's perfect offering. The way we enter into the Great Doxology during Mass will help us enter into the Divine Mercy Chaplet outside of Mass. There is an old saying: "Being good at one will make you better at the other." Well, in this case, praying one well with great fervor and intentionality will make you better at praying the other.

The "Fraction" of the Host at Mass

After the Great Doxology, the Mass transitions into the Communion Rite, which includes the Lord's Prayer, the Rite of Peace, the fraction of the Bread, and the distribution of Holy Communion. The "fractioning" of the Bread is the part of the Mass when, while the faithful are praying the *Agnus Dei* (Lamb of God), the priest has picked up the Most Blessed Sacrament in his hands and fractures the host in two, mingling a small part of the host with the Precious Blood. Praying the fractioning of the sacred Host relates more to the Divine Mercy Image than to the Chaplet; however, the two are united, as both take their source from Christ's perfect and eternal sacrifice to the Father.

The fractioning of the Bread points towards two mystical realties. The first is that by receiving the Bread of Life, many faithful are made one body (1 Cor 10:17). The second is that the fractioning of the Body of Christ can be considered analogous to the spear that pierced the side of Christ, from which blood and water gushed forth (Jn 19:34). As reflected in the Preface of the Solemnity of the Most Sacred Heart of Jesus, the Church has taught that the sacraments receive their power from the blood and water flowing from the pierced side of Jesus Christ. For raised up high on the cross, He gave Himself up for us with a wonderful love and poured out blood and water from His pierced side, the wellspring of the Church's sacraments, so that, won over to the open heart of the Savior, all might draw water joyfully from the springs of salvation.

During the fraction at the Mass, one can imagine the two rays depicted in the Divine Mercy Image emanating from the fractured Host. Our Lord Jesus Christ told Saint Faustina:

> The two rays denote Blood and Water. The pale ray stands for the Water which makes souls righteous. The red ray stands for the Blood which is the life of souls. . . . These two rays issued forth from the very depths of My tender mercy when My agonized Heart was opened by a lance on the Cross. These rays shield souls from the wrath of My Father. Happy is the one who will dwell in their shelter, for the just hand of God shall not lay hold of him. (*Diary* 299)

The fraction of Jesus is one of the most overlooked and under-prayed segments of the Mass. The challenge is transitioning from the Sign of Peace to praying, "Lamb of God, you take away the sins of the world . . ." Prior to the Sign of Peace, we are focused on Jesus on the altar, then for the Sign of Peace, we direct our attention to each other. At some point, as we exchange our Signs of Peace, our interpersonal interaction is disrupted by the proclamation "Lamb of God," and our attention is brought back to Jesus on the altar. Unfortunately, this is not a seamless transition. In our American Catholic Church culture, the Sign of Peace overflows into the "Lamb of God" prayer and many miss the opportunity to become dialed into this specific moment. However, when the Lamb of God begins, it should be a cue to bring your attention back to Jesus on the altar.

It appears that many of the faithful miss the opportunity to be very intentional about what they are saying and to whom they are saying it. When the *Agnus Dei* begins, the faithful's attention should snap and focus like a laser on Jesus in the hands of the priest. They should join their voices in speaking directly to Jesus the reality that He takes away the sins of the world, to have mercy on us, and to grant us peace. But also in this moment, they should use their imagination, in a mystical sense, to see the blood and water bursting forth from the fracture of the sacred Host and flowing over them and the whole world. If the blood and water from [Christ's] pierced side are the wellspring of the Church's sacraments, then it is reasonable to believe that the sacraments of the faithful in attendance are renewed and strengthened.

We can trust (Jesus, I Trust in You) that our sacraments of Baptism and Confirmation are strengthened and renewed; your sacrament of Matrimony is strengthened and renewed; and any cleric's sacrament of Holy Orders is strengthened and renewed. For each of us to see ourselves, our marriages, our families, or our priesthood penetrated, strengthened, and renewed by the pale and red rays that emanate from the fractured Host, we exercise the gift of faith and abandon ourselves and our intentions into Jesus's loving embrace. The key to praying this part of the Mass is to actively engage our imagination (based on what Jesus has revealed and the Church has approved) and unite it with our faith to surrender and allow Christ to enact real healing and conversion.

Below are a few quotes from Faustina's dairy to help develop the notion and effects of the "pale and red rays":

The Sacraments of Baptism and Penance purify the soul, and the Eucharist most abundantly nourishes it. Thus, the two rays signify the Holy Sacraments and all the graces of the Holy Spirit, whose biblical symbol is water, as well as the New Covenant of God with men in the Blood of Christ. (*Diary* 9)

O Divine Sun, in Your rays the soul sees the tiniest specks of dust which displease You. (*Diary* 71)

O Most Sacred Heart, Fount of Mercy from which gush forth rays of inconceivable graces upon the entire human race, I beg of You light for poor sinners. (*Diary* 72)

The two rays which emanated from the Heart of Jesus covered our chapel and the infirmary, and then the whole city, and spread out over the whole world. (*Diary* 87)

When [Fr. Sopocko] began to speak about the great mercy of the Lord, the image came alive and the rays pieced the hearts of the people gathered there. (*Diary* 417)

Conversation of the Merciful God With a Despairing Soul . . . **My child. You have a special claim on My mercy. Let it act in your poor soul; let the rays of grace enter your soul; they bring with them light, warmth, and life.** (*Diary* 1486)

Allowing ourselves to enter more fully into the fraction of the sacred Host will enable us to envision God's grace, not just touching us, but extending throughout the whole world.

Praying the Fraction for Fallen Away Catholics

Without exception, everywhere I go, entire families and faith communities have been ravaged by the devil and huge numbers of Catholics who have fallen away or abandoned their faith. The Church's participation in the COVID-19 lockdowns harmed the faith of its members in terrible ways. Through my missionary endeavors, it has been my experience that parish communities have lost 15 to 30 percent of their pre-COVID population. In addition to COVID, the world (and the devil) has offered our young people the gospel of comfort, instant gratification, life without consequences, a morality (and sexuality) of their own choosing, and the encouragement to worship the unholy trinity: me, myself, and I. It is as if this passage from the Letter to Timothy has been fulfilled in our time: "In the last days there will come times of stress. For men will be lovers of self, lovers of money, proud, arrogant, abusive, disobedient to their parents, ungrateful, unholy, inhuman, implacable, slanderers, profligates, fierce, haters of good, treacherous, reckless, swollen with conceit, lovers of pleasure rather than lovers of God, holding the form of religion but denying the power of it" (2 Tm 3:1–5). Each and every one of us has family members and/or friends who have received their sacraments but no longer practice the Faith. Praying the Fracturing of the Mass can help!

Two groups to consider when praying the fraction of the Eucharist are those who have received their sacraments but no longer practice their faith and those whose vocation (Holy Matrimony or Holy Orders) may be struggling or in trouble. Regardless, the prayer method is the same. As the priest initiates the Lamb of God, prayer begins. The goal is to stay absolutely focused on Jesus who is resting on the altar, and to speak to Him from the heart. As the priest picks up the sacred Host and begins the fractioning, imagine the individual(s) who have fallen away or are struggling sitting directly under the host, just centimeters away. Then, mystically see the blood and water that flows from the side of Christ gushing forth over and through them. See the pale ray, representing the waters of Baptism, washing over them and making them clean. Then see the red ray, representing the Precious Blood of Jesus, penetrating their heart, mind, and soul, infusing them with the Blood of Christ and giving them new life. It is my hope, my prayer, that when we pray like this, the two rays act like a set of defibrillator paddles that resuscitate people who are spiritually dead and bring them back to life; that the pale ray (water) washes them and the red ray (the Blood of Jesus) gives them new life. We have to act in great faith and to trust that God wants to do more than we can possibly imagine. When we pray like this, we can have confidence that someday, those who have fallen away or are struggling to live their vocations will have their breakthrough moment and echo the words of the centurion. "And when the centurion, who stood facing him, saw that he breathed his last, he said, 'Truly this man was the Son of God!'" (Mk 15:39).

Praying the Fracture for the Holy Souls in Purgatory

We would be far remiss if we neglected to apply the same principle and method of prayer to the poor souls in purgatory. It is as easy as following the same steps listed above but picturing yourself amongst the souls undergoing their purification. Maybe you are praying for one particular soul or just all of the souls in general. Regardless, imagine the two rays that emanate from the sacred Host penetrate deep into the imperfections of the soul or souls of those for whom you are praying. See instantly the power of God's purifying love, how a soul's purification is expedited by the direct encounter of Divine Love. Anyone who has read the lives of the saints who encountered the souls in purgatory knows that the souls are always asking for prayers and, more importantly, Masses to be offered for them. Next to having a Mass offered for a poor soul, this method of prayer (the fracture) and the Chaplet of Divine Mercy are two of the most powerful means of expediting the final purification of these souls. The souls in purgatory are totally dependent on the living to assist them in their purification. Please remember to pray for them.

Conclusion

Throughout my parish missions, I constantly tell people that if they only remember one thing I say, it should be this: "The most important thing in life is to get to heaven." Nothing else matters. God has made us for Himself and there is no other way for us to be satisfied. This book is not an exhaustive treatment on spiritual warfare but rather an overview, with some very specific and practical tips on how to engage and survive the fight. Be not mistaken: we are under attack. We do not get to choose whether or not we are in this war; there are no time outs or exemptions. We have two choices: fight and live, or lay down and die. Fighting and living means heaven. Not fighting by giving into sin and conforming yourself to the ways of the world means hell. One of our priests said it the best: "Nice people go to hell; the repentant go to heaven."

There are some in the Church who claim that there is reasonable hope that hell is empty and that everyone goes to heaven. This erroneous belief system is not only wrong but dangerous. We can be absolutely certain that there are people in hell because Sacred Scripture tells us so. Here are just a few instances:

> But as for the cowardly, the faithless, the polluted, as
> for murderers, fornicators, sorcerers, idolaters, and all

liars, their lot shall be in the lake that burns with fire and sulphur, which is the second death. (Rv 21:8)

And these will go away into eternal punishment, but the righteous into eternal life. (Mt 25:46)

And the devil who had deceived them was thrown into the lake of fire and sulfur where the beast and the false prophet were, and they will be tormented day and night forever and ever. (Rv 20:10)

And if anyone's name was not found written in the book of life, he was thrown into the lake of fire. (Rv 20:15)

For God so loved the world that he gave his only Son, that whoever believes in him should not perish but have eternal life. For God sent the Son into the world, not to condemn the world, but that the world might be saved through him. He who believes in him is not condemned; he who does not believe is condemned already, because he has not believed in the name of the only Son of God. (Jn 3:16–18)

In addition to these passages, there are various saints who have been shown visions of hell, including Saint Faustina:

Today, I was led by an Angel to the chasms of hell. It is a place of great torture; how awesomely large and extensive it is! The kinds of tortures I saw: the first torture that constitutes hell is the loss of God; the second is perpetual remorse of conscience; the third is that one's condition will never change; the fourth is the fire that will penetrate the soul without destroying it—a terrible suffering, since it is purely spiritual fire, lit by God's anger; the fifth torture is continual darkness and a terrible suffocating smell, and despite the darkness, the devils and the souls of the damned see each other and all the evil, both of others and their own; the sixth torture is the constant company of Satan; the seventh torture is horrible despair, hatred of God, vile words, curses and blasphemies. These are the tortures suffered by all the damned together, but that is not the end of the sufferings. There are special tortures destined for particular souls. These are the torments of the senses. Each soul undergoes terrible and indescribable sufferings, related to the manner in which it has sinned. There are caverns and pits of torture where one form of agony differs from another. I would have died at the very sight of these tortures if the omnipotence of God had not supported me. Let the sinner know that he will be tortured throughout all eternity, in those senses which he made use of to sin. I am writing this at the command of God, so that no soul may find an excuse by saying there is no hell, or that nobody has ever been there, and so no one can say what it is like.

I, Sister Faustina, by the order of God, have visited the abysses of hell so that I might tell souls about it and testify to its existence. I cannot speak about it now; but I have received a command from God to leave it in writing. The devils were full of hatred for me, but they had to obey me at the command of God. What I have written is but a pale shadow of the things I saw.

> But I noticed one thing: that most of the souls there are those who disbelieved that there is a hell. When I came to, I could hardly recover from the fright. How terribly souls suffer there! Consequently, I pray even more fervently for the conversion of sinners. I incessantly plead God's mercy upon them. O my Jesus, I would rather be in agony until the end of the world, amidst the greatest sufferings, than offend You by the least sin. (*Diary* 741)

Notice that "most" of the souls in hell did not believe in hell while on earth! Thus, the way the world is going, we have our work cut out for us. We need to save our own souls but also work to support the eternal salvation of our family members and friends, and, yes, even our enemies. Despite how much a person has hurt you or committed acts of evil against you, you should never wish the unending torments of hell against them. Rather, we pray for their conversion. We pray that God's mercy—the Blood and Water that flows from the side of Jesus—washes over them and brings tears of repentance to their eyes and a desire for a holy life.

Satan and his diabolic legions are fully committed to humanity's demise and destruction. That's the bad news. The good news is that the bad guys only make up one-third of the angels (see Rv 12:9). So, we have the remaining two-thirds of the angelic realms on our side, in addition to the saints, the Queen of Heaven, and the Holy Trinity. The deck is stacked in our favor if we so choose to align ourselves with the covenant family of God. On our own we are lost, but with God we can do anything.

I implore you to take the lessons of this book to heart and "fight like a knight" for the salvation of souls. Stay within the arms of Holy Mother Church! More than one commentator has observed that after forty days on the ark, with all those animals, it had to have smelled pretty bad, but the ark was still Noah's refuge. No matter how bad it gets, never leave Jesus because of Judas. Our souls need the sacraments of the Church.

In addition, develop your prayer life (have a routine that you stick to), where you not only spend time with God but win souls for the kingdom. Pray your Rosary and the Chaplet daily. At the end of our lives, as we breathe our last breath and stand before the judgment seat of God, we will never wish that we watched more YouTube, or social media, or spent more time at the office, or made more money, or had another pair of shoes. No, that moment will be one of absolute sobriety, where we will see our own soul as God sees it. There will be no excuses.

Remember the Divine Mercy Message is one for the end times. It is easy for these realities to feel overwhelming, but Jesus is inviting us to put our trust in the Mercy of God. Not man, not politics, not pharmaceuticals, not government . . . God alone. Trust in the promises of Jesus Christ that we read about in Faustina's diary.

> **I promise that the soul that will venerate this image will not perish. I also promise victory over [its] enemies already here on earth, especially at the hour of death. I Myself will defend it as My own glory.** (*Diary* 48)

These rays shield souls from the wrath of My Father. Happy is the one who will dwell in their shelter, for the just hand of God shall not lay hold of him. *(Diary* 299)

Whoever will recite it [the Chaplet] will receive great mercy at the hour of death. Priests will recommend it to sinners as their last hope of salvation. Even if there were a sinner most hardened, if he were to recite this chaplet only once, he would receive grace from My infinite mercy. (*Diary* 687)

I pour out a whole ocean of graces upon those souls who approach the Fount of My Mercy. The soul that will go to Confession and receive Holy Communion shall obtain complete forgiveness of sins and punishment. On that day all the divine floodgates through which graces flow are opened. Let no soul fear to draw near to Me, even though its sins be as scarlet. My mercy is so great that no mind, be it of man or of angel, will be able to fathom it throughout all eternity. (*Diary* 699)

The souls that say this chaplet will be embraced by My mercy during their lifetime and especially at the hour of their death. (*Diary* 754)

To priests who proclaim and extol My mercy, I will give wondrous power; I will anoint their words and touch the hearts of those to whom they will speak. (*Diary* 1521)

> When hardened sinners say [the Chaplet], I will fill their souls with peace, and the hour of their death will be a happy one. These souls have a right of priority to My compassionate Heart, they have first access to My mercy. (*Diary* 1541)

> Write that when they say this chaplet in the presence of the dying, I will stand between My Father and the dying person, not as the just Judge but as the merciful Savior. (*Diary* 1541)

> At three o'clock, implore My mercy, especially for sinners; and, if only for a brief moment, immerse yourself in My Passion, particularly in My abandonment at the moment of agony. This is the hour of great mercy for the whole world . . . In this hour, I will refuse nothing to the soul that makes a request of me in virtue of My Passion. (*Diary* 1320)

Jesus has made so many extraordinary promises through Saint Faustina. We should rejoice and embrace the four principles of exercising this devotion: confession, the Divine Mercy Image, Divine Mercy Sunday, and the Divine Mercy Chaplet. But most importantly, let us not forget the words at the bottom of the image, "JESUS, I TRUST IN YOU." The greater the faith we bring to these devotions, the greater the graces for us and for the world.

I hope you found this Divine Mercy message edifying and enriching. I truly believe that this is the most important message for our times. This devotion has an incredible power to draw a soul to God.

As the nations of the world fall deeper into darkness, confusion, and sin, it will be the light of Jesus Christ that breaks through that darkness and the bonds of sin. Jesus, the Divine Mercy, is our hope. If you ever feel overwhelmed or afraid, just gaze upon the Divine Mercy image and you will notice that it is Jesus who walks to you through the darkness and brings light, life, and love.

I encourage you my dear brothers and sisters: Do not be afraid! Set out into the deep of the ocean of God's Divine Mercy for yourself, for your loved ones, and for the world. Be bold; ask God to make you a great apostle of The Divine Mercy!

Examination of Conscience for Adults and Teens[24]

Prayer before Confession

Come, Holy Spirit, enlighten my mind that I may clearly know my sins. Move my heart that I may be sincerely sorry for them, honestly confess them, and firmly resolve to amend my life. Spirit of Wisdom, grant me to see the malice of sin and my ingratitude toward You, the all-loving God. Spirit of Fortitude, help me to make whatever sacrifice is needed to avoid sin in the future. Amen.

Did I deny or doubt God's existence?

Did I refuse to believe God's revelation?

Did I believe in (or use) horoscopes, fortune telling, good luck charms, tarot cards, Ouija boards, or reincarnation?

Did I deny that I was a Catholic?

Did I abandon the Catholic faith for any period of time?

Did I despair of or presume on God's mercy?

Did I neglect prayer for a long time?

Did I fail to pray daily?

Did I blaspheme God or take God's Name in vain, curse, or break an oath or vow?

---

[24] The Examination of Conscience is available as a free download at www.fathersofmercy.com.

Did I miss Mass on a Sunday or on a holy day of obligation through my own fault?

Am I always reverent in the presence of the Most Blessed Sacrament?

Was I inattentive at Mass?

Did I arrive at Mass late?

Did I leave Mass early?

Did I do unnecessary servile work on Sunday?

Did I disobey or disrespect my parents or legitimate superiors?

Did I neglect my duties to my husband, wife, children, or parents?

Did I fail to actively take an interest in the religious education and formation of my children?

Have I failed to educate myself concerning the teachings of the Church?

Did I give a full day's work in return for a full day's pay?

Did I give a fair wage to my employee(s)?

Did I give scandal by what I said or did, especially to the young?

Did I contribute to anyone's abandoning of the Catholic faith?

Was I impatient, angry, envious, unkind, proud, jealous, revengeful, hateful toward others, or lazy?

Did I give bad example, abuse drugs, drink alcohol to excess, fight, or quarrel?

Did I physically injure or kill anyone?

Have I had an abortion, or advised or supported an abortion?

Did I participate in or approve of the grave evil known as "mercy killing" or euthanasia?

Did I attempt suicide or physically harm myself?

Did I willfully entertain impure thoughts and desires?

Did I dress immodestly or provocatively?

Did I use impure or suggestive words?

Did I tell impure stories or listen to them?

Did I deliberately look at impure television, internet, plays, pictures, or movies?

Did I deliberately read impure material?

Did I perform impure acts by myself (masturbation) or with another (adultery, fornication, or sodomy)?

Did I marry or advise another to marry outside of the Church?

Did I abuse my marriage rights?

Was I unfaithful to my marriage vows?

Have I kept company with someone else's spouse?

Did I practice artificial birth control or was I or my spouse permanently sterilized (tubal ligation or vasectomy)?

Did I steal, cheat, help or encourage others to steal, cheat, or keep stolen goods?

Have I made restitution for stolen goods?

Did I deliberately fail to fulfill my contracts or to pay my bills? Did I give or accept bribes?

Did I rashly gamble or speculate or deprive my family of the necessities of life?

Did I tell lies? Deliberately in order to deceive or injure others?

Did I commit perjury?

Did I vote in accordance with a properly informed conscience, in a way consistent with the teachings of the

Church, in regard to the sanctity of marriage and of human life issues?

Was I uncharitable in thought, word, or deed?

Did I gossip or reveal the faults or sins of others?

Did I fail to keep secrets that I should have kept?

Did I eat meat knowingly on the Fridays during Lent or on Ash Wednesday?

Did I fast as required on Ash Wednesday and Good Friday?

Did I fail to receive Holy Communion during the Easter Season?

Did I fail to confess my sins at least once a year?

Did I receive Holy Communion in the state of mortal sin?

Did I receive Holy Communion without fasting for one hour or more from food and drink? (water and medicine are permitted)

Did I make a bad confession by deliberately not telling all the mortal sins I had committed?

Did I fail to contribute to the support of the Church?

Have I forgiven those who have hurt or harmed me or my loved ones?

The Ten Commandments

1. I am the Lord Thy God. Thou shall not have strange gods before Me.
2. Thou shall not take the Name of the Lord thy God in vain.
3. Remember to keep holy the Lord's Day.
4. Honor thy father and thy mother.
5. Thou shall not kill.

6. Thou shall not commit adultery.
7. Thou shall not steal.
8. Thou shall not bear false witness.
9. Thou shall not covet thy neighbor's wife.
10. Thou shall not covet thy neighbor's goods.

The Two Greatest Commandments

1. You shall love the Lord your God with your whole heart, with your whole soul, and with all your mind.
2. You shall love your neighbor as yourself.

The Precepts of the Church

1. You shall attend Mass on Sundays and on holy days of obligation and rest from servile labor.
2. You shall confess your sins at least once a year.
3. You shall receive the sacrament of the Eucharist at least during the Easter Season.
4. You shall observe the days of fasting and abstinence established by the Church.
5. You shall help to provide for the needs of the Church.

The Beatitudes

1. Blessed are the poor in spirit; for theirs is the kingdom of heaven.
2. Blessed are the meek; for they shall possess the land.
3. Blessed are they that mourn; for they shall be comforted.
4. Blessed are they that hunger and thirst for justice; for they shall be filled.

5. Blessed are the merciful; for they shall obtain mercy.
6. Blessed are the pure of heart; for they shall see God.
7. Blessed are the peacemakers; for they shall be called the children of God.
8. Blessed are they that suffer persecution for justice's sake; for theirs is the kingdom of heaven.
9. Blessed are you when people revile you and persecute you and utter all kinds of evil against you falsely on my account. Rejoice and be glad, for your reward will be great in heaven.

Three Eminent Good Works to Overcome Our Sinfulness

Prayer, Fasting, and Almsgiving.

The Evangelical Counsels

Chastity, Poverty, and Obedience.

The Seven Capital Sins

1. **Pride:** Preoccupation with one's own excellence or misery.
2. **Avarice/Greed:** Disordered desire for possessions; setting our hearts on material things; selfishness.
3. **Lust:** Disordered desire for or inordinate enjoyment of sexual pleasure.
4. **Anger:** Uncontrolled emotion which results in desire for revenge; holding resentment.
5. **Gluttony:** Putting the pleasures of the body (food, drink, makeup, Internet, TV, etc.) over the goods of the soul.

6. **Envy:** Sadness at the good of another.
7. **Sloth:** Bodily or spiritual laziness or neglect.

The Seven Capital Virtues

1. **Humility:** Acknowledgment of truth about God, oneself, and others.
2. **Generosity:** Doing actions for the benefit of others; selflessness.
3. **Chastity:** Proper integration of sexuality within the human person according to the mind of God and one's state in life.
4. **Meekness:** Gentleness of spirit that gives power of self-possession; governs anger.
5. **Temperance:** Moderation of the desire for pleasure.
6. **Brotherly Love:** Desire for the true good of one's neighbor, which leads one to act rightly toward him.
7. **Diligence:** Consistency in doing what is right.

Sins against the Theological Virtues

1. Presumption on God's Mercy.
2. Despair of God's Mercy.
3. Resisting and/or attacking the known truth.
4. Envy at another's spiritual good.
5. Obstinacy in sin.
6. Final impenitence (refusal to repent).

Sins Crying to Heaven

1. Willful murder.
2. Sodomy.
3. Oppression of the poor.
4. Defrauding laborers of their wages.

Being an Accessory to Another's Sin

1. By counsel.
2. By command.
3. By consent.
4. By provocation.
5. By praise or flattery.
6. By concealment.
7. By partaking.
8. By silence.
9. By defense of the sinful action.

The Works of the Flesh (Gal 5:19–21)

Immorality, impurity, licentiousness, idolatry, sorcery, hatreds, rivalry, jealousy, outbursts of fury, acts of selfishness, dissensions, factions, occasions of envy, drinking bouts, orgies.

The Theological Virtues

Faith, Hope, and Charity.

The Cardinal Virtues

Prudence, Justice, Temperance, and Fortitude.

The Corporal Works of Mercy

To feed the hungry, give drink to the thirsty, clothe the naked, visit the imprisoned, shelter the homeless, visit the sick, and bury the dead.

The Spiritual Works of Mercy

To admonish the sinner, instruct the ignorant, counsel the doubtful, comfort the sorrowful, bear wrongs patiently, forgive all injuries, and pray for the living and the dead.

The Gifts of the Holy Spirit

Wisdom, Understanding, Counsel, Fortitude, Knowledge, Piety, and Fear of the Lord.

The Fruits of the Holy Spirit (Gal 5:22–23)

Charity, Joy, Peace, Patience, Kindness, Goodness, Generosity, Gentleness, Faithfulness, Modesty, Self-Control, and Chastity.

How to Go to Confession

1. The priest will greet you.
2. The penitent says: "Bless me, Father, for I have sinned." You then say how long it has been since your last confession.
3. The penitent tells the priest his sins and briefly answers any relevant questions.
4. The priest will give you some advice and will assign you a penance.

5. The penitent will next pray the Act of Contrition (see prayer below).
6. The priest then gives the penitent absolution.
7. The priest will then say: "Give thanks to the Lord, for He is good."
8. The penitent responds: "His mercy endures forever." The priest will then dismiss you.

Act of Contrition

O my God, I am heartily sorry for having offended Thee and I detest all my sins because I dread the loss of heaven and the pains of hell. But most of all, because they offend Thee, my God, Who art all good and deserving of all my love. I firmly resolve, with the help of Thy grace, to confess my sins, to do penance, and to amend my life. Amen.

Prayer after Confession

Almighty and Merciful God, whose mercy is boundless and everlasting and of whose goodness the riches are infinite, I thank You because You have so graciously pardoned all my sins and restored Your heavenly favor.

I am awed by Your divine compassion and the incomprehensible love of Your Son, which has led Him to institute so gentle and powerful a remedy for sins. In union with all the gratitude that has ever ascended to You from truly penitent hearts, I proclaim Your merciful praises on behalf of all in heaven, on earth and in purgatory, for ever and ever. Amen.